May 17, 1996

Dear Ron & Terri —

May you Ron — be the "power"
supply and you Terri — provide
the tenderness as you begin
this great adventure together!
Congratulations —
WE love you both
(already!)

Michael & Leigh-Ann
McCool

x

THE
ENGAGEMENT
BOOK

WILLIAM L. COLEMAN

Tyndale House Publishers, Inc.
Wheaton, Illinois

ACKNOWLEDGMENTS
Many friends have helped by spending hours reading this manuscript.
My special thanks go to Mark and Doreen Olson, Cliff Jensen, Zandee
Nelson, and Clint and Cindy Petersen. I also want to thank Lois
Janzen for typing the book. Additional gratitude goes to my friend
Dr. Paul Welter for his suggestions in the revised edition.

The Engagement Book was previously published under the title
Engaged.

Front cover photo by Jim Whitmer

Unless otherwise noted, Scripture quotations are from *The Living
Bible* © 1971 owned by assignment by Illinois Regional Bank N.A.
(as trustee). Used by permission of Tyndale House Publishers, Inc.,
Wheaton, IL 60189. All rights reserved.

Dedicated to

Spencer Boone

Erv Nase

David Hamburg

Charles Bruynell

Tom Leader

CONTENTS

Preface   *9*

1   You Control Love   *11*

2   The Engagement Elevator   *23*

3   Good People Make Good Marriages   *33*

4   Friends, Relatives, and Old Girlfriends   *43*

5   The Fun of Marrying a Stranger   *53*

6   A Great Marriage   *63*

7   The "Hidden" Problem   *71*

8   Sexual Limbo   *81*

9   Love Communicates   *91*

10   Nine Things Your Partner Would Love to Hear   *101*

11   Getting Good Advice   *107*

12   Haunted Houses   *117*

13   Mixed Couples   *125*

14   Do You Want Children?   *135*

15   You Can Never Go Home   *145*

16   Married Sex Is Fun   *157*

17   What Is Your Inheritance?   *171*

18   Quick Tips   *177*

19   Weddings and Honeymoons   *183*

PREFACE

IT'S good to know some things never change. Couples are still holding hands and saying silly things. They walk in parks, buy crazy gifts, and see magic in rainbows. Love laughs at jokes no one else would think funny. Love can talk for an hour and never say anything.

Love is hope. Love says there will be a bright tomorrow because we have each other.

Eventually love looks for its peak in marriage. Maybe that's where you are looking now. This book is aimed at helping you give marriage the fantastic start it deserves.

As you read I hope you will gain good tools for the happy years ahead. Possibly you will be able to throw off a fear here or a myth there.

Above all else, I hope you can come a little closer to seeing how great God wants marriage to be.

With your eyes wide open, enter into one of the greatest experiences you can ever know. I think you will find life better together than any other way.

Thank you to the many who have written and called over the years to say how useful this book has been. Evidently this volume has helped couples launch satisfying and challenging marriages. My hope is that this updated edition will furnish guidance in making yours a fantastic and rewarding life together.

William L. Coleman
Aurora, Nebraska
1989

1

YOU
CONTROL
LOVE

LOVE is one of the most enjoyable mysteries in life. It can carry us higher than we ever expected to go. It can also immerse us in a whirlpool of uncertainty and frustration. Yet, for all its extremes, most of us wouldn't miss love for anything.

The majority of us will follow love until it eventually leads to a marriage altar, complete with candles and freshly cut flowers. Before we step over this threshold into a new life, we need to ask some helpful questions. How much of love is merely a passing emotion? How much is fad? Are we caught up in something we have not even begun to understand? What role does God play in the scenario? Is love even important to a marriage?

Love: Impossible to Define

If there are times when we feel confused about love, we shouldn't think we are alone. The author of Proverbs said there were four things he couldn't understand. You guessed number four! He couldn't figure out the growth of love between a man and a woman (Prov. 30:19).

I can still see Stan and Sue sitting in my office. They were grappling with the same "taffy" most of us have pulled. The more they stretched to understand their love, the stickier it got. Their problem seemed simple, almost ridiculous. They loved each other greatly. They were bright college students with excellent futures. Nothing seemed to stand between them and a thoroughly happy marriage—nothing except their own fears and confusion. They needed someone to talk with who would help them get a clear view of love.

The hundreds of thousands of Stans and Sues don't need a scientific dissection of love. Sometimes we become so academic we tear the tenderness out of simple passion. Love is more an art than a science. The fact is that you can't have 3.2 children. No family has 3.7 members. One-third of your engagement can't break up. You are a person and not an average.

Some things can be said with pinpoint accuracy. For instance, there are different kinds of love. Love for God, for our spouse, for our country, and for our dog may not be the same. Love is a renewable resource that may run low and later increase.

However, love is dynamic. It pulsates. It changes. Thank God, some days it's blind, deaf, and speechless. None of these qualities should change. Three cheers for moonlight and roses. Long live walks in the park and a tender touch. Who can ever forget a pair of eyes that once turned your knees to Jell-O?

But inside we all know this is only part of the picture. In order for love to last, it has to be more than a sunny feeling.

The Myth of "Falling in Love"

Certain facts must be rehearsed about love. Otherwise they are forgotten or distorted. How could anyone foul up something as basic to life as love? Through movies, books, divorces, greed, and unfaithfulness, we seem to manage. Fortunately, the Bible offers guidelines to get us back on course.

A young lady said, "I don't like what Tom says and I don't like what he does. Even my friends don't care for him. But I can't help it—I'm in love with him."

Her words convey what is probably the most misunderstood fact about love. Too many of us still think love is something we can never control. This simple mistake may do more damage than any other.

The fact is that love is stronger and more vital because we can ultimately control it. It is also the greatest guarantee that our marriage will last.

Track down love in the New Testament. The Bible commands me to love my wife, my neighbor, my enemies, and even God himself. How terribly unfair if I can't control love. I answer back, "But I don't feel a love for my wife. It isn't my fault." God's law still doesn't change. He tells me to love my wife. He knows I can control how I feel.

Many of us have been completely misled by the phrase "falling in love." It sounds like a sudden infection. Either love hits you or it doesn't. When it does, you can't do anything about it. If love misses you, your situation is just as hopeless. Many of us sit around waiting to see if the lovebug will bite.

Actually, some people do fall in love. We see someone from across the room, he looks great, our glands do a sudden rush, and *ding dang dong* goes our trolley. Nothing wrong with that. The initial feeling may last a few hours, a few months, maybe even a couple of years. But if that fall doesn't develop into something more substantial, you are probably in for a serious case of heartburn.

Life often seems simpler if we can blame everything on another force. That's why Satan gets accused so much. God also gets blamed for many things he didn't start. The same desire to escape responsibility has kept a chubby little fellow in a diaper alive—namely, Cupid. But the responsibility for love and its fantastic benefits rests squarely on our own shoulders.

Years ago, booklets that gave helpful information on love were popular. Titles promising magic formulas sold like heartburn tablets. People wanted someone else to make their decisions—maybe a referee to call them "out" or "safe."

The greater maturity is to accept the decision as ours. In the final analysis I must determine if I choose to be in love. Then I know no trick of fate has trapped me. I love because I choose to love. We hold our heart in our

Love is dynamic. It pulsates. It changes. Thank God, some days it's blind, deaf, and speechless.

own hands. No one can steal it. When I find that certain someone, I will give my heart to him or her with enthusiasm.

Will You Stay Together?

Ann was enormously in love. Her face sang. She had a sparkle like the diamond she wore.

"I don't know what it is," she said, "but when I look into his eyes, there is something that melts me."

What does she see? Why don't her girlfriends see the same thing? The only magic in his eyes is what Ann puts there. She sees something special because she chooses to love him.

This principle becomes more important with each passing year. After you have been married fifteen years, you might ask yourself, "Why do we stay together?" There may be younger people you find more attractive. Many of your friends may be divorced.

Why do you stay together? Because you choose to love each other. It is a conscious and voluntary decision. It is not based on a feeling that may shift with the next wind. It is based on a feeling you choose to stimulate.

Many young people protest. They insist love is not so easy to handle. You can't just turn it on and off like a knob on a television. Of course, they are correct. No passion is easy to control. But passion should not be allowed to run wild. We must not be angry without restraint. We cannot be joyful without boundaries. We dare not love without control.

It isn't easy to be the master over love. But it is essential. It is sane. It is filled with beautiful hope.

Could we love someone else? Certainly! Most of us have and could again. By selecting the person to love, we have drawn our boundaries. We will love no one else in the same way we choose to love this person.

Mature love is more than just feeling. I see someone walking at a shopping mall and I say to myself, *I could love her.* That is merely a feeling. I don't know her—her personality, her values, her tolerance. It is a gut-level feeling.

Lasting love is a passion that grows. The more we know

the person, the more deeply we love him or her.

There are a few people who are struck by love like lightning. The minute they see someone they hear violins. This usually happens only in the movies. As one writer has suggested, it *has* to be love at first sight in a show that only has two hours to run.

Surveys continuously support love by growth. The overwhelming majority say they did not fall in love all at once. They met a person and found him attractive or interesting. Whatever caught their attention made them want to learn more. Possibly they met the person again or went on a date. At any rate, something started to grow. The person became more interesting.

Some people are frustrated because falling in love isn't like a divine revelation or a heart seizure. Consequently, they wonder if it is even real. Such "falling" is a romantic dream that most of us have never experienced. But love that takes time can be the most enduring kind.

On the opposite side of the ledger, many instant romances have enormous difficulties. Dr. Paul Landis studied people who met and married within six weeks. Four out of five ended in divorce. There is much to be said for the time-and-growth approach.

Passion should not be allowed to run wild. We cannot be joyful without boundaries. We dare not love without control.

A Question of Expectations

Those who expect love to be automatic and instantaneous are often disappointed. It is more realistic to expect love to grow into full bloom as you live together in marriage. Then, rather than looking for an ideal experience, both lovers can expect to change and grow.

A couple who have been married for twenty years say, "We are more in love today than we were when we got married." It may sound like a polite bluff, but it also may be the exact truth. Both cohesion and adversity have caused their love to mature.

Ideally, a person enters marriage with a flexible attitude. He is not afraid of change. One year from now he will be a different person. He can hardly wait to see what the improvements are.

One of the most beautiful love stories in the Bible is about Isaac and Rebekah. They had never met each other.

Their marriage was arranged by Isaac's father and servant. Yet their romance was beautiful, partly because their expectations were high. Never having met, they had already decided to love each other.

"And Isaac brought Rebekah into his mother's tent, and she became his wife. He loved her very much, and she was a special comfort to him after the loss of his mother" (Gen. 24:67).

Contrary to popular belief, the first-century attitude toward divorce among Jews was wide open. A man could dismiss his wife for practically no cause. And yet divorce was rare. A Jewish author said the reason for so few divorces was simple: People didn't want to get divorced.

It is again a question of expectation. One couple has decided to try marriage to see if it works out. Another couple sees it as utopia. The realistic person sees it as a magnificent opportunity to grow in love and to change.

Wrong Reasons to Marry
Since love is so subjective, it is easy to fool ourselves. Many people marry for strange motives. One lady in ill health married a man for financial security; her husband wasn't wealthy, but he had an income. A high school graduate married so she would not have to face the working world. Her goal was to have a child and become a housewife as quickly as possible. Both women lived to wish they were single. Yet each had told herself she was in love.

Many marry a good body and call it love. One man said, "I was determined to marry the best body in the county. Two weeks after the wedding, the thrill wore off, and we realized we had nothing in common." Today they are divorced.

There are too many couples heading for the altar who do not really love each other. The pressures of life have pushed them together, and their lack of commitment may eventually catch up with them and completely gut their relationship.

Peg and Ron once had an exhilarating love. They were in their late teens and had gone together for two years. The first year of their engagement was immature but beautiful. Then the relationship started falling apart as their interests changed.

Peg's mother disliked Ron like taxes. (Actually, she hated him but couldn't use the word.) Mother was outspoken and tried hard to break them up. The second year they stayed engaged because they refused to let Mom win. Their love was gone, but they were welded together by a mutual enemy. They were determined to withstand her. Fortunately, they had enough sense not to marry. Unfortunately, some couples *do* marry because of mutual problems rather than mutual love. Read that sentence again!

Even love is not enough reason to get married. If I love a green Jaguar, that is no reason to buy one. I cannot afford the payments. My garage is too small. The car burns gas too greedily. And yet I lust for it greatly. I would love to have it. But it is a marriage that will never work.

We are individuals. Our love life will be like no one else's.

Many of us have met someone it would be easy to love. The person's attractiveness and personality are tremendous. However, we realize that his goals, interests, and idiosyncrasies would explode against ours. We decide to redirect our love. But some of it would have been nice; it really would have been.

There are several people you could love—more than one you could be extremely happy with. It would be thrilling to think there might be a "one and only"—a knight in shining armor who would one day appear on a hill. It only happens in commercials.

Testing Your Love

How do I know if I am in love? It's a frequent question in a highly romanticized society. The easiest answer has been an evasive "When the time comes, you will know." There is some truth to this old saw.

Probably a more accurate reply is, "When you find a person you could love, you will know it." True love is too personal to lend itself to magic formulas. Find a person to whom you can give yourself—whether you are a man or woman—and you have found someone you can love.

Too often we suffer by making too many comparisons. We want a love life just like our sister or brother has.

We hope for a romance similar to that of the couple in our neighborhood. Worst of all, we look for a movie romance.

We are individuals. Our love life will be like no one else's. It will not necessarily be better, but it will definitely be different.

Most of us have learned that love is no cure-all. The problems affecting marriage are obvious all around us. Thousands of marriages are dropping faster than the dollar.

Write this axiom where you can read it daily: "Love and marriage solve almost no problems." They intensify many difficulties, but they erase almost none.

Love is a joy. It will give you many things to smile about—and even make you laugh out loud. It must be the best tonic any of us can get without a prescription. But love has its boundaries and limitations.

A young man is unsure of himself and worries immensely. He is convinced that if only he had a loving companion, he would gain confidence. After the initial novelty of marriage wears off, he reverts to the same fearful person he was.

Some problems are too deeply ingrained to be eradicated by simple love.

Before we decide to give our love to a person, we should answer this question: *Can I be happy with this person if he never changes?* Too often people love an imaginary figure rather than the real thing. After we are married, we will get him to slim down. We know we can talk her into wearing contacts once we have settled down. We can live in the Midwest for a couple of years, but then I'll talk him into moving to the coast.

But what if he doesn't change? Can you live with that temper? Are you content to live a sedentary life? What if he doesn't change his mind about children?

Give your love to the person he is now, not to the prince you hope he will become. We all know examples of people who have changed drastically after marriage. However, don't bet your marriage on it. It is possible the change may be the opposite of what you had hoped.

Love is not an irresistible force. You can probably remember the summer you fell in love. For ten great weeks someone was the apple of your eye. When he left, your heart broke. Today you have pleasant memories, but it's definitely over.

Love is a controllable force. No one *needs* to fall in love. With eyes wide open, lovers can run and jump with real enthusiasm.

The Cable of Friendship

It helps a great deal to marry someone who is not only the throb of your heart but also your friend. Naturally, you need other friends, but if your spouse is not your friend, she will soon become a mere domestic companion. A domestic companion shares your house, children, and payments. A friend is interested in aspects of your life other than those within your house.

I was fortunate to marry my best friend. (But not my only one.) It is easy to confirm this. If I could spend an evening talking to anyone, I know who my first choice would be: my wife. There is an old French proverb that says: Select a partner you can talk to intelligently for the next fifty years.

Statistics indicate that those who know each other well before they get married have the most enduring relationships. They have taken time to test the soil. Is it a good place for love to grow?

Up until this commitment, most young people have only engaged in floating love. They have loved one person for a while and then possibly someone else.

The prospect of married love becomes another matter. This love finds its anchor in commitment. The two of you agree to nurture and strengthen a love for the rest of your lives. No previous love has reached this peak.

For most of us, love is essential. We want to know someone cares. When we are up, we want a special someone to know about it. When our hopes cave in, we need somebody to help us dig out.

Love gives me a special value. It says I am worth something. Somebody thinks I am just a little clever,

Before we decide to give our love to a person, we should answer this question: Can I be happy with this person if he never changes?

maybe attractive, and certainly important. Merely having that special person makes a drastic impact on my personality.

It isn't uncommon to see many loves fizzle out. They run strong for a short distance, but there isn't enough to sustain them.

John and Marcia suffered from love fatigue. The only thing they had in common was that they both loved John. (It isn't as novel as we might like to think.) Marcia gave and gave and gave. At first she thought she was supposed to. She even believed the Bible taught her that her only role was to please John. After having this kind of relationship for a couple of years, Marcia was worn out and decided to throw in the towel.

Others will establish their love on a mutual career. This may be especially true of a couple starting a business. It is also frequent among Christian ministers and missionaries. When the career becomes frayed, so does the love. It is common to find a couple in career trouble who are also in love trouble.

Probably there is no stronger cable than simple friendship to hold love together. The partners don't have to share everything. They don't need to be inseparable. He might go backpacking, while she never cares to go. She loves to bowl, and he has never picked up a ball. More important, they just like to be with each other.

Their values, religion, and mental pursuits have something in common. Even their fears may be similar. They can talk, confide, and dream together. Who is the person you would most like to talk with over coffee? If something tremendous happens, who do you want to call? Usually you call your best friend. Fortunately, your best friend is most often the person you love.

A Fantastic Partnership

Since we control love, we want to give it carefully. We don't hand it out for the moment. Hopefully we won't distribute it quickly for something that catches our eye. We look specifically for a potential friend and lover.

"Live joyfully with the wife whom thou lovest all the

days of the life of thy vanity, which he hath given thee under the sun" (Eccles. 9:9, kjv).

The fact that you control love is the greatest guarantee your marriage has. Suppose ten years from now you fall in love with someone at the office. If you can't control love, your life and perhaps that of someone else will become a mess. What can you do? Will you divorce your partner for your new love? Will you see the other person on the side or pine away in your heart? No. No. No. Because you control love, you will stop loving the person at the office. The decision and power are yours.

As long as you accept your responsibility in love, no one can fracture your marriage. You will have a fantastic partnership because you are in control.

Talk It Over

1. What are three reasons you are in love with the person you want to marry?
2. If you could change two things in that person, what would they be?
3. How has your love for each other grown since you first met?

The fact that you control love is the greatest guarantee your marriage has.

2

THE
ENGAGEMENT
ELEVATOR

"SOME days I really get scared."

His wedding day was coming closer. Like a train chugging through the mountains, the puffing smoke was in view.

"You ought to be scared." Charlie's reply shocked him. "This is one of the most important decisions of your life. Everybody gets shook."

Charlie summed it up fairly accurately. A few people never become frightened or second-guess their decisions to marry. The other 90 percent shake in their boots sooner or later. Somewhere along the line we experience everything from absolute ecstasy to numbness, from staring into space to cold feet. Most people wonder if they are really going to go through with it.

Second Thoughts

"I wonder if I'm weird." He was an engaged university student. "I have so many ups and downs about this engagement, I start to think I'm not stable."

He has a lot of company. The fact is, almost half of those who get engaged call it off before the final bell rings. Some call it off more than once. Nearly one out of two swim around, grope, swallow buckets of water, and finally go under.

Ron is a prime example. He said, "I'm glad someone told me that everyone gets scared. I was ready to climb out the window. It helped to know that I'm not the only one who feels like running away."

If you have second thoughts, you are definitely part of the majority. It isn't uncommon to have a couple wrestle over the engagement on the very night he proposes. She will take the ring; she won't. "But what if this happens?" "Shouldn't I talk to my parents one more time?" "I'm still thinking about what my sister said." The sentences come in colorful varieties, but they all amount to the same thing. The person is often happy, frightened, and confused—all at the same time.

The important thing to remember is that most of the time engagement is an elevator. Expect the ups and the downs. They will eventually go away. Some of the best marriages started out with months of the willies.

It is sad to see some couples collapse merely because they don't recognize this. If the engagement doesn't run smoothly, they are sure the marriage is doomed. This is not true.

We become victims of our own idealism. We expect love to rise above the bumps of life. Often it does. Love can fly with the eagles. I have never experienced any happiness like being in love. But love also hits the pavement, bounces, and fractures.

Some couples sail into rough weather. Instead of calmly handling the problem, they are shocked by the fact that they have the problem at all. They didn't expect to doubt their love. They didn't expect to want to run. Rather than accepting doubt as a passing, natural feeling, they become obsessed with it. Consequently, they never recover. One day the engagement dies a cruel death.

Thank God for broken engagements. I can remember couples who were obviously not suited. It was evident to everyone but them. The conclusions bore it out. Their marriages became alley fights. Some great people walked into terrible marriages.

Once engaged, you don't have to stay there. But don't

bail out because of the normal ups and downs. You may miss something beautiful just because you got nervous.

"I just gave up trying to figure it out," said one man. "The more I tried to understand it, the more confused I got. I finally said to myself, 'I don't understand how I feel, but I'm going through with it, just believing it will all work out.'"

His marriage survived because he knew it was normal to feel confused.

Some chapters in this book are aimed directly at the difficulties of marriage. Discussion questions are usually geared toward this emphasis.

What about Problems?

By the time we are warned about all the potential problems in marriage, we are bound to get a distorted view. We look at all the hazards, the pitfalls, the dangers. No wonder we become afraid.

With all the stress on these factors, it is a wonder anyone gets married!

Many people are just thrilled with being married. They enjoy the companionship, the love, the sex, the planning together, and the children.

"I don't want to get married," said a pretty teenager. "After what I've seen of my parents, it's a lousy trip."

What a shame! Some have watched broken hearts on television and heard songs of wrecked marriages. Some have read depressing novels and watched their parents fight.

Someone should stand up and scream, "Stop!" Millions of married couples are as happy as mice in a granary. They wouldn't have missed marriage for anything.

When we focus on the problems, we create problems.

An engaged couple becomes confronted with a disagreement and they often imagine the world has ended. They are convinced their marriage won't work. It's a bad way to begin.

Concentrate on your dreams. Most of them will come true. Read that sentence again. Most of them will come true.

You will spend quiet evenings alone in your own living

Most of the time engagement is an elevator. Expect the ups and the downs.

room. There will be soft music playing on the stereo. There will be a career that will grow and develop. You will spend vacations at your favorite place. Not all of your dreams will come true, but most will. Doesn't that sound great? It would be a shame to dump those dreams because of a few misunderstandings now. Most of life will not be lived under these conditions or this strain.

I walk in the strength of the Lord God. I tell everyone that you alone are just and good. O God, you have helped me from my earliest childhood—and I have constantly testified to others of the wonderful things you do (Ps. 71:16-17).

What a powerfully upbeat statement about God and life. Hold on to it. There are too many good things happening to concentrate on the setbacks.

Many engaged couples have this strength in common: They can laugh together. Even the ones who were in deep distress knew they had a sense of humor. I remember one couple on the verge of separating. The differences in their backgrounds, careers, dreams, and even theology seemed irreconcilable. But they still kidded. They teased. There was a sparkle in their eyes. In your heart you knew it would work out. Underneath their stack of problems, they genuinely enjoyed each other.

If you take it all too seriously, you may lose it.

The Shorter the Better

Sometimes the longer the engagement, the more chance there is for difficulties. Young people are often asking the same question: "How long should a couple be engaged?" The answer is simple: The shorter the engagement, the better off most couples are.

Recently Betty told me she had accepted a beautiful ring. Tony gave it to her at a great restaurant in town. Her smile was so wide it was causing stretchmarks. Unhappily, they don't expect to get married for three or four years while she finishes school.

I hope it works. Unfortunately, the pressure to live

together and the tension of being "half-married" usually take a painful toll.

But you thought people had to get to know each other. You are correct. Statistics demonstrate that the better two people know each other, the better are their chances for a happy marriage. One hundred percent right.

However, the period of engagement is *not* the best time to get to know each other. Date each other for one, two, three, ten years if you want. But once you say, "We are going to get married," do not pass go and do not collect $200. Take the shortest route to the altar. If you are not prepared to get married for a year or more, don't get engaged. It works for some but not for most.

People have all sorts of grandiose schemes as to why they must wait before they get married. If you are not ready to get married, it is generally unwise to get engaged.

"We want to work for a while and then get married." In most cases it isn't worth it. If you are rich enough to get engaged, you are rich enough to get married. Get married and then work for a while.

"I have another year at college before I get married." Great! Then take another nine months before you become engaged. Absence does not necessarily make the heart beat faster.

"I want to get married, but we have to wait until my mother's health is better." That is a strong reason, but the answer is the same. There is no way to guess how long your mother will be sick. Don't get engaged if you are not ready to get married.

Some will object: "My sister was engaged for two years, and they have the ideal marriage." They are the exception and not the rule. Get to know each other before you are engaged. Engagement periods are unusual situations and are not best geared for getting to know each other.

I heard it again just a month ago. A newly married friend said, "Tell them to keep the engagement short. It can really be tough."

How long you are engaged does depend on the person. But certain guidelines are true. The shorter the engagement, the better for most.

Concentrate on your dreams. Most of them will come true.

A large number of engaged couples are actively engaged in some form of premarital sex. Many are unhappy and guilt-ridden. Others are trying to justify their behavior but honestly find it hard. Their actions and their feelings are easy to understand. Shorter engagements could greatly alleviate this problem.

It is hard to tell whether this generation is looser sexually than any previous one. The Puritans had tremendous problems trying to control sexual activity. Despite their famous laws, adultery and pregnancy out of wedlock were common. Possibly other generations were just as active, but they didn't have as much open publicity.

Let's hear it for sexual activity. But let's put it inside marriage, where it belongs. Then you can exercise your freedoms and joys to your heart's content.

Dust Storms

There are a number of storms to expect during engagement. It is important to remember they are just that—passing storms. Engagement is the season for them. After they have moved through, life will go on. Often we are better off for the experience.

One of them we can call a dust storm. It covers everything and causes everyone to choke. Dust from the parched earth can even creep through closed windows.

Engaged couples often smother and choke each other. It is natural to want to be together. Pity if you don't. You think, even dream, about each other. Most couples hang around each other constantly. Don't be surprised if sooner or later you get tired of the constant companionship. You are still in love; you have merely begun to smother.

Maybe you would like to go shopping alone. You want to go to a ball game with your other friends. If you feel that way, it doesn't mean you don't love each other. After you are married, you will sometimes feel the same. Back off some. Your love can handle it. A few evenings apart may be a beautiful tonic.

Hailstorms

By the time you adjust to the dust storm, the hailstorm will probably arrive. Hailstorms bring a million marble-sized problems down at once. Wedding arrangements are a good example. The strain can be severe.

Many couples have thoroughly enjoyed their elaborate weddings. Others have come to me afterwards and said, "Tell young people to elope." Different strokes for different folks.

"I ended up in the middle," said Becky. "My parents wanted a large wedding. My mom picked out the cake and the invitations. She thought she was being so helpful— going with me everywhere and paying for everything. But it wasn't what I wanted. On the other side, I have Bob. He wants a quiet wedding—just our families in the minister's living room. Between Bob and my mother, I'm about to go nuts."

Becky is in a hailstorm, and it's all coming down on her head.

Sometimes before a wedding is over, some very rude remarks are said. Occasionally, there are severe wounds among relatives.

If you have open-minded, cooperative parents, thank God for them twice.

The object of a wedding is to get married—happily. Don't let it become an agony. Hang loose on the arrangements (see chapter 19). They are often not worth the strain. If something about them really aggravates you, let it be known early. Tell yourselves repeatedly, "No sets of candles, no corsage, and no wedding is worth hurting the two of us."

Rainstorms

You can also expect a good rainstorm. Everything will become overcast, dull, and damp. Don't be surprised.

It is hard to keep a bubbling love during an engagement. Ron explained it to me this way; "Just let it happen. I'm tired of all the questions I ask myself. *Is she the right one? Is this really love? Should we go through with this large wedding?* Man, I'm numb. Just let it happen."

He was suffering from engagement fatigue. Ron was tired, discouraged, gloomy. He was still in love, but it was masked under all the prolonged pressure. As the saying goes, it was raining on his parade.

The period of engagement is not the best time to get to know each other.

Don't interpret the doldrums as a lack of love. The barometric pressure is getting to you. You don't have as much zip on a cloudy day. Try to recall good times. Remember that evening alone in the restaurant? The glowing candles, the look on his face, the gentle touch of his hand? It will all be there again. The rain will pass. Everything will look brighter and greener. Don't let a few dips and doubts rattle you.

Thunderstorms

If all these other storms pass over, a thunderstorm will get you for sure—the kind that rumbles loudly and frightens everyone. It's just a passing noise, but it's still scary.

Are you ready to live intimately with someone each day? This is a genuine fear. It disturbs a large number of engaged people. Maybe you have lived with brothers and sisters. Possibly you have had roommates. Marriage is a different dimension. Do you want someone to get to know you this closely?

Your partner is going to discover your personal habits. Do you snore? What about your hygiene? What if you aren't a good sexual partner? Can you compromise with your mate's life-style? Does she go to bed early and you late? Can you stand each other's uncamouflaged temperament?

Will you continue to love each other? You can hear the fears rolling like thunder. Will this be something you can't handle?

These reservations are not abnormal. They will pass. In most cases, the better we know each other, the more we love each other.

"I know my wife's little habits now. I love them," one happy husband said.

Unless you have some bizarre or weird habit, the two of you will mesh beautifully. Do you eat raw onions in bed? Do you chew tobacco in church? If either of these is true of you, you have some adjustments to worry about.

Every year a million people become married and adjust well. Many of them stay married for fifteen, twenty-five, or forty years and have a great time. You will, too.

Don't let the rolling thunder scare you. When you get

to know each other better, you will love each other even more.

If you think you are the exception to this, you are not. We have amazing adaptability. Add love and it is marvelous what a couple can do. Despite whatever reservations you have, you are normal. Love really will win out.

Weathering the Storms

Once when Jesus was out on the lake in a boat, a gigantic storm came up quickly. It threatened to destroy the vessel and everyone in it. He decided to speak to the storm.

"And he arose, and rebuked the wind, and said unto the sea, Peace, be still. And the wind ceased, and there was a great calm" (Mark 4:39, KJV).

The storms of engagement can be just as threatening. Tell them to calm down. They can be destructive. The smart couples keep them to a minimum. They remind themselves that all storms pass. When they are over, life can go on with tremendous happiness.

Not every engagement is worth redeeming. Some couples have constant and irreversible storms. They really should bail out—immediately. It is too bad to have to say that, but it is true.

However, most engagements are worth the effort. I see too many couples at the breaking point for no good reason. They heard a rumor. They have picked up some lousy advice. It isn't the magic cloud they thought it was. They are tired. Eventually they go their separate ways, thinking the marriage was never for them. Maybe it wasn't. But maybe they lost something just because they became confused.

One of my favorite couples, two college students, were so enjoyable and interesting. I think of them often. We got together several times because their engagement was on the rocks. They loved each other; neither denied it. They had fun together. It was obvious.

What was their problem? She had heard a sermon someplace, and he didn't live up to it. The minister had said if a young man is this or that, don't marry him. She took the minister's opinion as gospel.

Then her sister said you should never marry a man if

I see too many couples at the breaking point for no good reason. Maybe marriage was never for them. But maybe they lost something just because they became confused.

he won't do this or that. She loved her sister, and that advice really bothered her.

Here were two excellent Christian young people being torn apart for no good reason. It was a thrill to see them finally get married.

Engagement can be a dizzy elevator. It's a passing part of life. It will usher you into a beautiful marriage.

Talk It Over
1. Have you wondered whether or not to stay engaged? Can you tell your partner what has bothered you?
2. Is anyone creating pressure on your engagement or wedding? How can you best handle this person?
3. What stands between you and your wedding date? Do you want to move it closer? Is there some reasonable way to move it up?
4. What is the most fun about being engaged?

3

GOOD PEOPLE MAKE GOOD MARRIAGES

MARRIAGE solves almost no problems. This sentence should be printed at the top of every marriage certificate. Too many look at marriage like baking soda: It can do practically anything.

It is important to know what it can and can't accomplish before the organ starts playing. Marriage offers some basic joys. You will have someone who cares. Loneliness will be diminished. Sexual pleasure will be available but sometimes with frustrations.

However, most personal and personality problems will be intensified and not eliminated in marriage. If you expect wedding bells to cure your hangups, back up and look again.

Good people make good marriages. The more you can smooth off your rough edges now, the greater chance the two of you have for tremendous happiness.

When Personalities Stay the Same

There was a young man whom everyone liked. He was intelligent, had a great sense of humor. People were drawn to him.

Greg became engaged to a most unpleasant character.

*GOOD
PEOPLE
MAKE
GOOD
MARRIAGES*

*page
34*

He loved her and rationalized Ellen's behavior. After all, she was under a great deal of pressure. Between going to school and planning a wedding, she was bound to become irritable.

Greg's friends never mentioned why, but they stayed away more and more. Ellen was genuinely unbearable.

Greg and Ellen celebrated their first wedding anniversary by filing for divorce. Greg's hopes were not based on fact. Marriage could not change Ellen. It only intensified her characteristics.

The formula has almost mathematical precision. Selfish fiancés make selfish husbands. Insecure fiancées make insecure wives. Don't fantasize that you are marrying someone you are not.

Someone has a terrible temper, but his love-struck partner rationalizes it away. After they get married, she tells herself, she will be able to calm him down. She is taking a great risk. In most cases, the temper will stay. Many times it will become worse in a close relationship.

I'm not saying this to frighten anyone. But it has to be said to help us face reality. The first few months after marriage will probably be full of bubbling joy. Then your personalities will settle into their normal tempo. Both of you will begin to revert to your real behavior. If you married a good person, he will be exactly that. If you united with an unstable personality, he will revert almost certainly.

Don't fool yourself into believing your partner will become Mr. Nice Guy. He will be basically what he is now.

Ask yourself the question once more. *If my partner never changes at all, can I be happy with him?* Don't get married until you answer that question.

All of us know someone who has been tremendously changed by marriage. I think of a man who married an outstanding woman. She changed him for the better. His clothes changed. He joined a bowling league, became a leader in several organizations, and seemed to enjoy life far more than he had before.

These were things he always had wanted to do, but he couldn't get off the ground. His personality is still the same. He was a good person—and he still is.

Marriage is a normal part of life. Sometimes we talk as if it were different. If you are a kind person, considerate, sharing, a good listener, and someone who feels good about yourself, your chances for a sound marriage are excellent. But these are the same qualities that make solid people. Marriage is not a separate world.

Taking a Close Look

Divorce courts are filled with couples who married to solve problems. She wanted to get away from her parents. He was dependent on a bottle. She was a manic depressive. He couldn't control his passions. They thought marriage was the cure.

One of the saddest women I ever met was one who had married for money. Not big money, as most of us might imagine. She was just looking for simple support. Her health wasn't good, and she felt she couldn't work. She met a lonely man, and a marriage of convenience seemed like a good solution. Before long she wished she was in the bread line at a street mission.

Selfish fiancés make selfish husbands. Insecure fiancées make insecure wives.

Again, I'm not writing to frighten you (well, maybe some of you). Rather, I'm calling you to take a close look at yourself as well as your partner.

We can change. We can change ourselves, and God can change us. The more good alterations we make before we are married, the better the chances are for a healthy union. Read that again.

A young lady said to me in defiance, "I can't help it. I am what I am." Thank God that isn't true.

Read this verse slowly to yourself: "When someone becomes a Christian he becomes a brand new person inside. He is not the same any more. A new life has begun!" (2 Cor. 5:17).

The potential for change is there. Sometimes adjustments can be made by our own determination. Other times a couple may need professional attention. You may have to ask God to ship in a few miracles directly.

A solid marriage does not depend on your ability to be perfect. However, the smoother your machine is running, the better the factory will go.

Here are some questions to help you start taking a

closer look at the areas you may need to change. Add your own queries to this short sample.

How do you handle anger? Do you brood until everyone around you is uncomfortable and depressed? Do you hold onto anger for days or even weeks? Or are you the other extreme? Do you have to break things, hit people, or put on a physical performance?

Either extreme will take its toll on a relationship. Practice talking about your anger, and keep short accounts. Never let it carry over into the next day (see Eph. 4:26).

For years we may have practiced harmful behavior. Today let us start practicing constructive behavior.

Do you get more fun out of giving or getting? A healthy person likes to receive. However, if we see our major goal as getting, we establish a self-centered relationship. This will become painful later. To have one partner completely deny himself makes a one-sided marriage.

Practice giving more than you get. What is your main concern at Christmas—what you will give or what you will receive (see Acts 20:35)? After you have been married a year, your attitude toward giving will make an enormous difference.

Do you have to win? Does it tear you up when things don't go your way? Look at the little things in your life. How do you feel if you lose a game of Pictionary or Scrabble?

A young wife said, "We have learned not to play games together. My husband can't stand to lose. If I beat him, he's impossible to live with." I wish I had a dollar for every woman who has said this.

Maybe you take yourself too seriously. It is no fun to share with someone who must always be right. This is a good definition of *spoiled.* You can change that by relaxing and learning to appreciate sharing. Love does not demand its own way (see 1 Cor. 13:5).

How do you cope with jealousy? When your partner gets compliments, does it tear you up or make you happy? What will happen if your wife has a job making more money than you? Do you become upset when your partner does things with his friends?

Suppose your wife wanted to join a women's bowling

GOOD
PEOPLE
MAKE
GOOD
MARRIAGES

🌹

page
36

league. What if your husband wanted to play on a local basketball team? Since you can't participate, will you insist your partner not go either? Will you let him go but pout about it for a week?

Your reactions now will give you a good clue. Are you jealous and overly possessive today? Unless you practice letting go, your smothering will continue into marriage (see James 3:15-16). Don't confuse jealousy with love.

Are you a trusting person? Developing trust can be hard, especially if your parents have had trouble. Possibly you feel insecure. You are constantly afraid you will lose everything. Do you want to carry these feelings into your outstanding relationship?

Practice giving more than you get.

Some people have made fear part of their personality. They don't trust anything that is going well. If life is running smoothly, they are certain tragedy is about to hit. They expect trouble. By expecting it they frequently cause it.

If your partner calls to cancel a date, do you distrust her reasons? When she says she loves you, are you suspicious that she is pretending?

Feelings of distrust are understandable, especially if you have been hurt often. However, you must begin to improve your trust. Love calls for us to completely accept our partner. The degree to which we refuse to trust is the exact degree to which we will fracture our relationship.

Talk to your partner about your feeling of distrust. Your partner may be able to put it to rest bit by bit (see Prov. 31:10-11).

Is your partner guilty of "gaslighting"? In the movie *Gaslight* the husband, played by Charles Boyer, turned everything back on his wife, Ingrid Bergman, causing her to doubt herself. He would say things like "Did I say we were going out tonight?" or "Did I say I'd be home at six o'clock?" Unwilling to own up to his shortcomings, he tried to destroy her sense of self-confidence.

Accusations like "You planned it on the wrong night" or "You failed to remind me" may indicate a need to escape responsibility. If that pattern exists, your partner may have to be confronted over his or her attitude and behavior.

Is he or she the kind of person who needs to hurt others? Unfortunately, there are partners who get their sense of power by causing turmoil and agony in the person they supposedly love. They like to create pain and confusion to "teach a lesson."

For every man or woman who likes to play this torturous game, there seems to be a partner willing to marry him. Look closely at the twisting game your proposed partner is playing. Is there something sick about the trend his behavior takes?

How's your sense of humor? This sounds easy because everyone believes he has one. Can you laugh at yourself? If not, you just flunked. Do other people do funny and strange things, but not you? If not, perhaps you take yourself too seriously.

When your partner messes up, humor will become even more important. What will happen when she burns dinner? Will you throw a fit? Make a speech? Or comfort her?

Some of the best marriages have partners who can laugh at themselves. It will really come in handy one day when you are broke, the car radiator leaks, and your favorite chair breaks.

Practice laughing; it is good medicine. Flatly refuse to marry anyone who cannot be cheerful and laugh at himself (see Prov. 17:22). Flatly.

Make your own list of rough edges. What would you like to smooth out? What changes or improvements would you most like to see in your partner? Now is the time to start working.

The Courage to Change

In premarital counseling I always try to ask, "If you could change one thing in your partner, what would it be?" Almost every time this question brings good response. "He always wants me to make the decisions." "She puts me down a lot." "He always talks about old girlfriends." "She asks questions and won't let me answer."

Try it with your partner. Each of you agrees to share one or two things you would like to change in each other or yourself. Then make suggestions on how you can help.

GOOD
PEOPLE
MAKE
GOOD
MARRIAGES

page

38

It sounds great to say, "I wouldn't change one hair on your head." All right, leave her hairdo alone, but a couple of trait changes might be good insurance on your marriage success. You are doing her a fantastic favor.

What kind of person would you like to be? If you could map out the type of personality you want most, where would you start? Why not start there now? Tell yourself three things you are not doing as well as you would like. Now aim for those goals. As you move toward them, you will become happier with yourself. In the end both of you will be happier with your marriage.

Knowledge alone cannot make a compatible marriage. Learning about married life in itself is not enough. After you read the books and take the counseling, one question remains all-important. What kind of person are you? No amount of information will overcome a failure here.

Experts in social behavior are deep into theories of what ruins marriages. Is it a mobile society? Working women? Urbanization? Confused roles? Financial pressure? Unrealistic sex expectations? Close living quarters?

One authority would have none of this. Cutting through all the dialogue, he said simply, "Basically, people are getting divorced because of selfishness."

Could it be that simple? A common human weakness as basic as this? Marriage is made up of people. People with good qualities make good marriages.

100 Percent-100 Percent Marriage

In the past we have been guilty of sex prejudice. The job of changing was relegated to the woman. The male supposedly had an inalienable right to be whatever he was. A husband's personality was considered fixed. If the wife did not fit exactly, it was her place to change until she matched.

Thank God, that day has ended. No longer does the husband make the sole decision on where to live. No longer does he alone set the pace of their social life. No longer does he invest the family money without consulting his spouse.

To consider your wife's feelings in making decisions was once considered a sign of weakness. A man thought

What will happen when she burns dinner ? Will you throw a fit ? Make a speech? Or comfort her ?

he should tell his wife what to do. If she was a good woman, she would obey.

Do you want to marry a man who must prove his manhood by bossing his wife around? If he needs to do this, how fragile is his manhood?

The biblical concept is not this rigid. It offers choices to the female that we are only now starting to admit. Read about the virtuous woman in Proverbs 31. She is a woman who has more liberty than most husbands today are willing to allow. The virtuous wife runs a business. "She goes out to inspect a field, and buys it" (Prov. 31:16). Don't marry until your partner has read this chapter slowly.

A good partner is not afraid to give his wife freedom. Let her express herself. What interests mean the most to her? Would working outside the home be healthy for her and the family? A sensitive partner does not try to map out his spouse's life and nail it down. Husbands and wives must be equal partners.

I can remember a first-class couple who were shooting sparks over the issue of freedom. First, he told his story.

At the end of a day he was tired, ready for a hot meal. If he wanted to go out, watch television, or work a puzzle, he expected his wife to be available. After all, this is why he got married.

That sounded simple enough. It's the same principle we have been working on for hundreds of years.

Marie also had a point, and her husband wasn't really considering it. She wanted more than to be lost in her husband's personality. Her part-time job gave her a sense of added worth. The two organizations she belonged to gave her the chance to contribute.

How much freedom can you allow your partner? How much freedom do you want? Do your future marriage a favor and discuss this soon.

It isn't just a question of the wife accommodating her husband. Can the husband also accommodate his wife? The first rule of submission is submitting to each other (see Eph. 5:21).

A marriage relationship has to be based on affection and consideration. It isn't like running a factory or a schoolyard.

GOOD
PEOPLE
MAKE
GOOD
MARRIAGES

page
40

This is why a fifty-fifty marriage is a poor concept. It says, "I'll do my half if you do your half." All this does is draw the line at which you will fight. It defines limits but is without compassion.

Far better is a 100 percent-100 percent marriage in which each partner says, "I'm going to give this my all." Mature partners aren't afraid of this type of commitment because they both love and trust each other.

You are not afraid to give your all to your mate. You are confident your partner will do the same.

The Greatest Qualification

Sometime when you are asking yourself what kind of a partner you will make, read 1 Corinthians 13:4-8. It is the world's greatest description of love. Take a brief survey of what love does and apply it to your coming marriage.

Love is patient. It doesn't push a partner where he doesn't want to go. Love waits while a spouse thinks things over. It knows when it shouldn't bring up a problem.

Love is kind. Its behavior is gentle. Love doesn't believe being coarse or crude is cute. It not only hears what is said but also hears what is meant.

Love is not jealous. When your spouse beats you in bowling, you are glad for her. When someone shakes her hand, you are as happy as if the person were shaking yours. (Besides, you will win next time!)

Love is not proud. It doesn't have to puff up like a frog. If a partner disagrees and selects the wrong road, love doesn't rub it in. It doesn't crow when it's right.

Love is not selfish. A loving partner calls home when he knows he will be late. Love withholds its sex drive when the time isn't right. Love lets her pick out the wallpaper—then praises the choice.

Love is not rude. It remembers when to say thank you. Love helps pick up the paper clips a partner dropped. Love never repeats a spouse's conversations. Love never jokes in a way aimed to hurt a partner.

Love doesn't demand its own way. Love is mature enough to give in. It lets a spouse select the restaurant, then eats with gusto. Love waits quietly while a partner shops. (At least for the first hour.)

An old French proverb says: Select a partner you can talk to intelligently for the next fifty years.

Love is not irritated and touchy. It doesn't have a trigger temper. It listens to criticism. It takes some friendly kidding. Love doesn't tell mother-in-law jokes.

Love doesn't hold grudges. It has no notebook in which to keep old accounts. After the problem has been discussed, love never brings it up again. After an argument, love always rubs feet in bed at night.

Love isn't happy when its partner is hurt. It isn't glad when a partner gets chewed out. Love isn't happy when a friend criticizes a partner. Love wants to see the other be a winner.

Love is loyal. Love doesn't tear down, it builds. When it knows a spouse was wrong, it gives a hug anyway. When love has nothing good to say, it stays quiet.

Love always believes. During a difference, it always believes its partner first. Love is blind and is glad it is. If a spouse says she was kidnapped by a flying saucer, a loving partner asks how high she was taken.

Love expects the best. When dinner isn't ready, love assumes a partner couldn't help it. When one of you comes home late, love knows there was a good reason. Love wants to believe you threw out its old shirt by mistake.

Love never fails. Money, youth, and motorboats all fail. Waistlines stretch, teeth vanish, eyes weaken. Skin wrinkles, heads bald, arches drop. Love and love alone never gives up.

Love is profound and simple at the same time. Marriage isn't so complicated if we apply basic human love. The same qualities that make a good person make a good marriage.

Talk It Over
1. Do you have a history of distrusting either men or women? How did it develop?
2. What is your view of the value and status of women? In the home? In society?
3. How close to equality are men and women?
4. Who will make the "major" decisions in your marriage?
5. Do you picture yourself as a partner or as a benevolent boss? Explain.

GOOD
PEOPLE
MAKE
GOOD
MARRIAGES

page

42

4

FRIENDS, RELATIVES, AND OLD GIRLFRIENDS

MARRIAGE is change. Most of the changes will be for the better, and you will enjoy them. A few will hurt, but they have to be made. To expect and accept these changes in a relationship is a good indication you are mature enough to marry. If you try to keep every relationship with friends and parents the same as before, you are in for an explosion.

You are going to get to know your partner more intimately than anyone you have known before. You haven't known a brother, sister, friend, or parents this closely. You are going to be united not only physically but also mentally, emotionally, and spiritually. In a few years you will find yourselves thinking alike. Often you will know what your mate is going to say before he says it. When she hurts, your heart will break. When she succeeds, your heart will leap with joy. It's fantastic. If you think you are melting into "one flesh" now, just check a few years away. Many couples even start to look alike!

This is part of the greatness of marriage. When you are around a beautiful person, some of that beauty rubs off. It has to, just from the fallout. If you married an ugly personality, after a while you start to pick up the uglies.

Personality changes personality. Thank God! That is why he injected so many good people into our lives.

This is why you are marrying someone who has humility. If you marry a person who is stuck on himself, he doesn't appreciate change. Since he is already perfect, he sees no need for alterations.

Only fools marry brick walls. Walls are immovable and cannot be improved. Brick walls expect you to change to match their personality.

The smart partner knows his mate is good for him. He goes into marriage saying, "Marriage will change me. I am ready to make changes and improve." If he says this, throw an armlock on him and take him directly to the altar.

Because marriage means change, there is one scene you can almost bet on. Somewhere down the line (and maybe not far), you will be sitting in a corner sucking your thumb. You will be saying to yourself, "I always have to give in. I change 90 percent of the time, and she only changes 10 percent."

This type of thumb pacification is also known as self-pity. Expect it. It comes and goes. Normally, it is a tremendous exaggeration, but don't be surprised by it.

What about Friends?

If you move a train east from Des Moines toward Chicago, two changes have to happen. You become closer to Chicago but farther from Des Moines. You cannot move closer to Chicago and remain close to Des Moines at the same time. The same principle exists in marriage. An intimate relationship with my new partner will change close relationships I had with my old friends.

For a year I had a close relationship with an excellent friend. We were both single, had a great deal of free time, and floated around together. Don and I would go to the beach, eat out, or just bum around. The minute he was married, that relationship changed. He no longer had the free time. There was now a new and outstanding personality in his life. If we had kept as close a relationship as we had had before, it would have been at the expense of his new marriage. To get closer to Chicago he had to move away from Des Moines.

This was a healthy, normal change.

Paul was the opposite. He had two close friends, and the trio owned a racing car. It was a demanding hobby. They raced twice a week and worked on the blue bomb three other nights.

When Paul married, he stayed in Des Moines. He visited Chicago. He even kept his luggage there and popped in for meals. But there was no doubt where his real home was. Paul wanted his marriage partner to be a satellite—to orbit around his world. There would be no melting of personalities.

This is not the type of change most of us want. It is terribly unhealthy.

As always, the Bible holds this change in excellent balance. In marriage she becomes more like him and he becomes more like her. The two change to become one.

"That the husband and wife are one body is proved by the Scripture which says, 'A man must leave his father and mother when he marries, so that he can be perfectly joined to his wife, and the two shall be one' " (Eph. 5:31).

If you marry someone who is not mature enough to expect change, you are buying into an Excedrin headache. Check that again.

This doesn't mean you have to throw all of your old friends off the back of a train. Frequently, you keep some old friends and add new ones. It merely means adjustments have to be made.

Couple-Crushers

Two types of friends are couple-crushers. The first is the close friend who demands all of your time and energy. Your new partner takes absolute priority. Old friends must be pared down to size.

Your new mate must feel free from competition. If you consistently would rather be with old friends than with her, she will become puzzled.

You cannot move closer to Chicago and remain close to Des Moines at the same time. The same principle exists in marriage.

The second couple-crusher is the personality conflict. Once in a while an old friend will drive a new mate into spasms. The offense could be his conversation, clothes, body odor, feet on the coffee table, or any other of thousands. If your mate cannot cope, then your course is clear. Your old friend has to be controlled or eventually eliminated. Often it will happen naturally. Sometimes it has to be encouraged.

Maybe you can keep all your old friends. Terrific. A few can. The important thing is to tell yourself up front: My new relationship is more important to me than any other in life. I will let no other relationship hurt this one. If I do, I am a fool.

Old Girlfriends and Boyfriends

This leads us to former girlfriends and boyfriends. Where do they fit into this new picture?

In almost all cases, they don't fit.

There are exceptions. I hear of an old girlfriend who becomes the new wife's best friend. I also hear of someone who finds a paper bag filled with one hundred dollar bills. It seems that I hear of both equally often.

One rule of thumb can be used concerning keeping old flames around: Don't. It is too difficult for both new partners to handle the situation well. Most often your mate will feel threatened by your old flame. Not always—only 999 times out of 1,000. When this doesn't happen, the reverse often does. You start leaning too much on your former heartthrob.

I know one man who keeps an old girlfriend close. She has never gotten over him, so it is no simple friendship. He loves the attention and uses his girlfriend or his wife to get whatever he wants. There is probably no sexual activity between the husband and his old flame—just excessive attention. All three of them need their clocks checked.

But staying away from old flames isn't the only way to please your partner. Most mates aren't thrilled at *hearing* about former friends either. Some husbands enjoy describing old girlfriends. This can be cruel sport. The smart partner doesn't bring them up. Your mate probably wants to know who they were. Maybe she wants details. However, it is certain she doesn't want too much information and absolutely not too often.

Live in the present. The past probably wasn't as interesting as you imagine it anyway.

Chuck was one young man who had to make a tough decision. He had an old friend who happened to be female. There was never anything serious between the two except they were real pals. Several girlfriends came and went, but Michelle was always there.

After Chuck was married, Michelle continued to write, and contact seemed harmless to both of them. It wasn't harmless to Chuck's bride. When Michelle offered to come and visit, it was more than the bride could handle. Chuck loved his wife too much to hurt her. He knew he had to back off from the relationship with Michelle.

Relationships change after marriage. They must always change in one direction—to reassure love and unity between marriage partners.

One rule of thumb can be used concerning keeping old flames around: Don't.

Relatives

What is the most difficult of the changing relationships? The hardest change—bar none—concerns our parents and in-laws. Consistently, this is a major problem among married couples. It is hard to switch from being a dependent to being an independent.

First, stop and give a silent salute to the thousands who have no trouble here. There are some terrific parent-couple complements. Don't believe all the jokes you hear. Some couples would not trade their parents for anything.

If we start to accept all the stereotypes, they have a way of coming true. By expecting trouble we often cause it.

The parents who seem to get along the best are the ones who have this basic principle in line: They raised their child to get rid of him. This is the purpose of having children.

Those who raised children to keep them have created puppets with tight strings. Often adult children have to reach up and cut those strings to walk on their own. The cutting is frequently painful but, in the long run, it is the only chance to stand on one's own feet.

Smart parents have moved the young person along steadily. They have given the youth increased freedom as he has grown. Their hold has become less and less choking. They have been aiming for the day when he will be free and flying on his own.

They have understood the Scriptures well: "A man must leave his father and mother when he marries" (Eph. 5:31). When the time comes, everyone is prepared for him to leave.

Leave and Cleave

Jim and Nancy have just this type of marriage. They feel fortunate not to live too close to either set of parents. They can visit but are not continuously camped on each other's doorstep. If they ask their parents for advice, they usually get it. Sometimes the parents politely refuse even then. They merely assure Jim and Nancy that either way they do it is perfectly fine with them.

The parents are helpful and friendly. They have no desire to butt in even once. If they are going to make a mistake, it will result from holding back.

Jim and Nancy have only appreciation for parents. They don't quite understand what other couples are complaining about.

A healthy parental relationship is possible. It just doesn't occur often enough.

One of the saddest young women I know has never been set free. Today she is married and has three children. After years of training, she also has an excellent career. Yet if you know her, one thing becomes obvious. Everything she does is aimed at pleasing her mother. She keeps a spotless house, dresses impeccably, keeps the children completely in tow. There is nothing wrong with any of these things except that she lives in constant fear of her mother. Any derogatory remark from Mom and she crumbles. Mother has never set her free and never intends to. Cindy's husband also lives daily with the ghost of a living mother-in-law.

Resolve to avoid the same mistake. Raise your children to get rid of them.

A Parent Problem

We are discussing a parent problem and not just an in-law problem. Often we imagine it as an in-law problem because we do not see our own parents clearly. If our parents do something wrong, we are likely to be understanding. We have seen them this way before and have learned to accept them. When our mate's parents do the same thing, we object.

Keep the perspective sharp. It is a parent problem, and the solution needs to occur between parent and child. If your parents are making life miserable for your mate, it is better if you talk to your parents. Don't expect your partner to correct his in-laws. Crossing those lines usually only adds to the hostilities.

The hottest spot in the parent problem lies between a mother and her daughter-in-law. The hot wires that hit the most are female. I am not bigoted; that is just a fact.

Even this is not an in-law problem. The son should resolve this by talking to either his mother or his partner. It isn't reasonable to expect the wife to correct her mother-in-law. The mother has no business correcting her daughter-in-law.

Expect to have a great relationship with each other's parents. If you look for a fantastic experience, you are far more likely to get one.

Rules of Thumb

The smart couple will pledge to keep a few simple guidelines.

Never live with parents unless one or both of you are in a wheelchair. Even then, try not to do it.

Margaret agrees now. When she first got married, she and her husband were in love but broke. They moved in with her parents. She told me, "Tell couples not to do it. It just doesn't work."

Parents have final say in their households and may find it difficult to stay out of their married childrens' lives. Likewise, married children will not be able to be themselves with authority figures under the same roof.

If you can't afford to set up housekeeping, you can't

We borrow money from our parents. We park our kids at their house. Then we throw up our hands and scream, "Why don't they stay out of our lives?"

afford to get married. It doesn't take much money to become a couple. Live modestly, but live alone.

Don't accept gifts with strings. Parents like to be kind. We have two beautiful chairs in our living room that were a gift from Pat's mother. We have great parents. But *never* have they tried to tell us how to raise our children. They don't even suggest what we do with our lives.

Wayne had the opposite experience.

"Sure, I don't like what her parents say. They are always screaming about how we treat the kids. They don't like what I do for a living. But what can I say? They have given us every appliance in the house."

What could he say? Don't get yourself into that wedge. Some kindnesses are terribly cruel.

Don't dump on parents. Many parents never asked to interfere in the lives of their children. We borrow money from them. We park our kids at their house. We carry off half their furniture and their popcorn popper. Then we throw up our hands and scream, "Why don't they stay out of our lives?"

I have talked to good parents who didn't ask for this. Their children follow them around like shadows and then complain about being smothered.

You're too smart to do that.

The Question of Obedience

Change is almost always difficult. The change in our relationship to our parents is no exception. One day you belonged to your parents. Today you don't. Engagement continues that separation. The transition isn't easy.

Six persons are directly affected by most marriages: a couple and four parents. In order for the crossover to be smooth, all half-dozen must accept it equally. That's asking a lot.

Maybe this is why the Bible said it four different times (Gen: 2:24; Matt. 19:5; Mark 10:7-8; Eph. 5:31). When a person gets married, he leaves his parents.

The majority of us grew up learning to obey our parents. Some were more successful than others. Still, this was the theme. It was correct and helpful. How does this relationship change when we become married? Obey drops out, but honor remains.

"Children, obey your parents; this is the right thing to do because God has placed them in authority over you. Honor your father and mother. This is the first of God's Ten Commandments that ends with a promise" (Eph. 6:1-2).

Honor is respect. If our parents have advice or counsel to give, we appreciate it. Their experience is valuable, and we are foolish not to listen. Wisdom is a gift usually reserved for those with years behind them. There are times when we will seek out this advice. This could save us a carload of agony.

If you grew up in a dysfunctional family, honoring your parents is no easy matter. Space doesn't allow us to adequately discuss this problem, but we would recommend you see your pastor or a Christian counselor or seek out a support group.

The line is drawn when it comes to the question of obedience. A partner who doesn't understand this difference is not completely ready to marry.

When you marry, you do not marry an entire family. You marry each other. Other relatives become satellites, but they are not part of the marriage. Only two people become one, not six or a dozen.

Ann was a typical victim of "marrying" a family. When she stopped by to see me, she was on her way to pack. Her husband, Dale, was completely tied to his parents. He still believed he had to obey them.

Both of Dale's parents were physically healthy. They worked every day and attended social functions. Mother wanted the family at their home on Sundays. Dad wanted Dale to help him work on Saturdays and a couple of evenings a week. Whenever Ann tried to change this routine, Dale became hot. There was no way he could go against his parents' wishes.

Dale wasn't ready to get married. He expected Ann to marry an entire family and melt her identity into theirs. Now she was looking for luggage.

If you marry someone who has not cut the cord, you

To separate yourself from your parents is neither unloving nor inconsiderate. It is natural. It is maturing. It is beautiful.

will spend many unhappy days mumbling to yourself. To separate yourself from your parents is neither unloving nor inconsiderate. It is natural. It is maturing. It is beautiful.

Smart parents store up for themselves. Not just financially, but in every area. They develop their own interests, hobbies, friends, and emotional supports. When their children leave, these parents are not gutted. Their lives and happiness did not depend entirely on their children. The families that are built mainly on child-satisfaction are heading for a letdown.

Whatever the level of changing relationships, they can be exciting. Above all else, they are normal and healthy. Each one is a stepping-stone in the rich maturing of your life.

Talk It Over
1. What kind of parents do you have?
2. Are you prepared to *leave* them and *cleave* to each other?
3. Is there a close boyfriend or girlfriend you need to discuss? Who? Why?
4. Do either of you have a friend whom your partner does not appreciate? Can you help bring them closer? If not, how can you help resolve this difficulty?

FRIENDS,
RELATIVES,
AND OLD
GIRL-
FRIENDS

page
52

5

THE FUN OF MARRYING A STRANGER

DO you like adventure? Do you find it stimulating, even exciting? Do you see something new as interesting or as a threat?

Marriage may be life's greatest safari, an amazing trip into a new territory filled with beauty, wonder, and change. The attitude you take into this trip will make a fantastic difference.

The two of you have taken time to get to know each other. By now you have a fair idea of what makes your partner tick. Immediately after you are married, you will begin to unfold the rest of the map. You won't like every side road and gully you see, but most of it will be everything you hoped for. This rule far outweighs the exceptions.

Marriage Makes a Lousy Science

Why do you want to marry this character, anyway? Have you ever thought of why you two strangers decided to get together?

One group of surveys says you picked each other because opposites attract. You are going to get married because you are different. Another battery of surveys says you gravitated toward each other because you are similar.

This is handy. You can select either group you want and agree with it.

The fact is, marriage makes a lousy science. If nine people out of ten marry because of loneliness, you could be one of the nine, or you could be the one. Don't try to study marriage to death.

Why did you select the mate you plan to marry? What is attractive about him physically? Which part of his personality do you find most appealing? There is no special key that applies to everyone. Your key is like no one else's.

Sometimes two extroverts make the worst possible partners. They may be always screaming and stomping out on each other. The next two extroverts may be as happy as two penguins on a one-foot ice drift.

We do not have to pair off into extroverts and introverts. Don't fall for the old "type A cannot be happy with type B" formula. Too many young people have missed magnificent partners because they believed these so-called guidelines.

Our basic premise remains unchanged. The same qualities that make good people make good marriages.

Some marriages are terrible from day one. Every young couple needs to admit this.

A couple came to talk about getting married. It was obvious they were a mismatch. It wasn't because of introvert-extrovert conflicts; the male lacked the qualities essential to a good person. He was inconsiderate, demanding, paranoid, gruff, and self-centered. He was not just flunking marriage, he was flunking humanity.

Later he had marital problems. Baloney. He had humanity problems, and they were affecting his marriage.

There used to be an old adage floating around that insisted, Don't marry people from broken homes. The theory was that it was a chain reaction; broken homes would break homes. This is true only if people are statistics and categories. Fortunately, we are flesh, blood, brains, and nerve endings.

I know tons of good people who come from broken homes. Don't fall for prejudices and stereotypes. Christians should be the first people to see past these blinders.

Some young people have lost beautiful potential

partners because they listened to nonsense. Aunt Agnes always said you should never marry a man whose parents are divorced. Mom says I should look for a quiet man because I talk all the time. You've heard that anyone who marries a foreigner will regret it.

Mark them all false. You are people, not statistics.

The doors of marriage will swing open and the two of you will go waltzing in, wide-eyed, eager, and flexible. You'll find you can hardly wait to discover new things about the person you love. With this attitude you can't go wrong.

The fact is, marriage makes a lousy science.

Depth Charts

Begin on day one to make a depth chart on your mate. Recently, I saw a depth chart of Chesapeake Bay. It is easy to see the shallow spots to avoid when sailing. You can just as readily note the deep places where you can sail ahead.

Over time these depths will change. Sand will shift and new paths be worn away. Mark these down in your mind also.

Making a depth chart is not the same as conniving. There is nothing deceptive about it. Anyone who has worked for a boss has done the same thing. When the boss is in a foul mood, everyone stays clear. If he is telling jokes, they crowd in with requests.

Your mate's day will have certain high or low points. A smart partner mentally charts them. There are some situations that he dreads. A good navigator backs off when she sees her partner getting near those. Good mates read the charts well. They sail more smoothly and go around less often.

One partner was always frustrated. She got home an hour before her new husband. During that time she drank a cup of coffee, started supper, and often arranged her evening.

At six o'clock the light of her life came dragging in the door, looking like a wet raincoat. Glad to see him, she came on like a game show host. How was his day? Did he want to see her new shoes? Could he go with her later to the shopping center?

Her bowed-back beau always seemed so negative. He didn't want to see anything and he didn't want to go anywhere. Sometimes she felt sorry for herself for marrying such a deadpan grouch.

One day the facts hit her like a mosquito in a motorcycle race. After dinner he was pleasant, conversant, and practically creative.

She realized she had one hour ahead of him to gather her wits and energize. She marked it on her depth chart. Six o'clock is a sandy reef. Wait until the craft is farther from shore.

Some partners will find evening breezes the best. The two of you are sitting in the living room, and all the necessary things are done. It is easy to talk without tension. Calmer decisions can be made.

The next couple will find those evening chats the pits. It's late. Your mate doesn't think straight. Don't try to solve inflation, the oil crisis, or the bank overdraft now.

Most partners can mark this on their chart immediately. Don't give bad news late at night. Sometimes the news can't wait; but when it can, hold it.

If the transmission falls out of the car, midnight is probably not a great hour to shock him. If there is a gas leak in the basement, any hour is a good one to speak up. When there is a choice for bad news, don't pick late.

Timing is only the beginning of this chart. My wife and I play a game over baked potatoes. She likes them; I don't. They are so easy to fix. Pat manages to slip them in once in a while.

By now she has learned the ground rules. If she has done me a special favor during the day, I can count on a baked potato. (This is the severest form of cruelty.) What else can I do but smile and try to shovel the spud down?

This is clearly unfair. But she has learned she can sail here when the wind is right.

Charting your partner is not the old female slave concept. This approach said the wife had to knuckle under and do whatever the husband wanted.

This outlook on marriage is dying and never should have lived. The wife-as-slave idea was never biblical. The wife was never intended to be wallpaper (see Eph. 5:21-22; Prov. 31).

Two-way Soundings

Charting is absolutely a two-way street. She takes soundings on him, and he takes soundings on her.

For instance, husbands can mark down a day or two of low tide each month. Most wives sag during their menstrual period. Learn to chart this by experience. Women are extremely different. One wife will barely blink during it. Other women can be bedridden.

The biggest help is to communicate. All a wife has to say is, "This is a bad time of the month for me." It can prevent many problems. Husband then knows to back off for a couple of days. Without this information some strong arguments often erupt.

At the bottom of their imaginary chart, wives should write this note: "Most male illnesses are terminal." There are exceptions to this rule, but they are too rare to consider.

Many men can't stand being sick. When the flu knocks them out for a couple of days, they become impossible. He is convinced he is going to die. He tells his wife where the insurance policies are hidden. He calls for the chroniclers to record his last words.

For many young wives, this is a startling experience. Husbands who are sick will expect to be babied, fed, and flooded with attention. They frequently fall into lapses of self-pity. Somehow men can't imagine Joe Montana with diarrhea.

Ride this storm out patiently. Your neighbor goes through the same thing.

In most cases, we marry people who operate on different levels. Our mate will probably talk at a rate different from us. Don't try to remake the person. Learn to appreciate him. Silence has its healthy qualities, and we can see its value by watching our partner. Great conversation can be rich medicine also. Listen to your mate and appreciate the strength of sharing.

As time does its work, many couples become more like each other. The one will probably become more

Your mate's day will have certain high or low points. A smart partner mentally charts them.

talkative, the other slightly more pensive. But don't force it. Learn to love the difference rather than demand imitation. A mature partner doesn't insist on compliance. She understands the need for personal freedom and variety.

John told me about his timing problem and how he matured in his response to it. He was the type who loved to stay up late. Too much sleep drove him goofy. A good book or a late show was his idea of a relaxing evening.

His wife, Lori, acted as if electricity was evil. Why would anyone want to stay up late? If the sun went to bed, people were supposed to follow soon.

Their experience is common. During the first month both partners tear up the stairs trying to get to bed early. (It isn't that they are sleepy.) But as time passes, their normal patterns emerge. Often partners do not have the same sleep pattern. Differences frequently lead to frustration or haggling.

John and Lori decided it was smarter to chart each other than to fight. They kiss good-night and part happily when Lori goes to bed at ten o'clock. At midnight John climbs the stairs at his own pace.

They also mix respect and compliance. On some nights John goes to bed early. The next night Lori might stay up a little longer. Frequently, John will go to bed and make love and then get up for an hour.

Each married a stranger, but they are getting along fantastically. Instead of saying "Happiness is to be like me," they have charted each other. Now they do it their own way—and each other's way.

This is called marriage.

How to Be a Great Romantic
Men have traditionally found two-way soundings harder to accept than women. Many of us thought women were to make depth charts on us, but we never made charts on women. After all, the purpose of marriage was to make the husband deliriously happy.

Our entire society is maturing. Now we know one of the purposes in marriage is to please each other. Men will be charting women and not just the other way around.

This isn't a new concept. The Bible taught it thousands

of years ago: "And you husbands, show the same kind of love to your wives as Christ showed to the church when he died for her" (Eph. 5:25).

Old King Nebuchadnezzar understood the principle. He greatly loved the woman who owned his heart. After they got married, he noticed she was becoming melancholy. Her vim and vigor were gone. He patiently inquired, and she finally told him the facts. The new queen missed the beautiful mountains of her home country. She didn't know if she could ever get used to the dry plains of Babylon.

The great romantic went right to work. He ordered mountains built. They were to be near the palace and have gigantic trees and lush gardens. The king would set his lover's heart singing or break the national budget trying.

Nebuchadnezzar's little valentine became one of the wonders of the world—the Hanging Gardens of Babylon. All because he gave his heart to a little girl from the hills.

Make yourself a promise before you begin to chart your partner. Promise you will never brood over the changes you make in yourself. Some foolish partners make sacrifices for their mates and then spend years pouting about it. Love that is grudging is not love at all.

If a man agrees to buy a house in the suburbs because it's his wife's dream, he should not then turn it into a weapon. Can you imagine the grief that would result if for years he brings up the house whenever there is a disagreement? After a couple of seasons of being beaten over the head by it, the wife begins to see the old domicile with lackluster eyes.

Sometimes generosity is more painful than denial. The person inflicting the misery usually can't see it. He says, "Well, I gave her what she wanted, didn't I?" No! Not if it was given like a vise, to be slowly tightened around her heart until it aches continuously.

Giving in is an act of love. But if it is done incorrectly, it becomes cruel.

The Bible lays out a beautiful pattern for giving in. It says God loves a cheerful giver (see 2 Cor. 9:7). I translate it "a giggling giver." Be a *hilarious* giver. "Would this make you happy? Baby, this is just what I want you to have."

Learn to love the difference rather than demand imitation. A mature partner doesn't insist on compliance.

Lessons in Giving

When you give your partner gifts, there are several guidelines to keep in mind. You want to give in love and not just in awkward patches. So run each gift idea through this quick checkup.

1. *Give what your mate wants, not what you want.* Giving can be terribly selfish. One year I gave my wife a baseball glove for Mother's Day. It was a charming act on my part, but I could be accused of selfishness. Fortunately, she understood how badly I needed someone to hit fly balls to.

Selfish giving takes some of the shine off a gift.

2. *Gifts are not trades.* There is a place to barter in marriage, but gift-giving is not it. You may strike a deal on vacations. You will spend one week in Florida and one week in Cleveland. That is a fair deal.

Don't make every gift a deal—it then ceases to be a gift. You give to your partner whether you will receive in return or not. (Strangely, this type of giving almost always receives.)

3. *Give a nice gift.* Your partner has been asking for a camera, and you are tired of hearing about it. Don't buy a cheap one to get her off your back. Make her even happier than she had hoped.

Never give a gift with a twist of defiance.

4. *Be a happy giver.* Nothing increases the value of a gift as much as a warm, genuine smile.

Let Your Partner Breathe!

Too many of us grew up with brothers and sisters. We learned how to give in and fight at the same time. Marrying a magnificent stranger may call for a realignment of our emotions.

Promise your new partner you will give him plenty of room for creative breathing. Not only is this person a stranger to you, but he is in many ways a stranger to himself. There are many areas in which your mate has never ventured. He would like to. Whenever possible, encourage him to branch out.

Some people are extremely proud that their mate never differs from them. There is no creative breathing. She thinks like him, acts like him, even enjoys the same shows as him. This can be good as long as one of them has not erased the personality of the other.

A few years ago there was an important issue on the ballot in our town. A handsome new museum was built by private contributions, but there was no money left to support it. We were asked to vote on whether or not the county should assume the cost.

The day of reckoning came. I voted to support it. My wife voted against. The measure failed.

What was the sense of voting? All we did was cancel each other out. But it was terribly important. She felt free to breathe her way, and I breathed mine.

She chooses her career. She takes her classes. She selects her wallpaper. As far as possible, a partner should be free to pursue his or her interests.

We have a close friend who enjoys country music. He has a collection of old Hank Williams records, which proves he is hopelessly addicted.

He married a young lady who has been well trained in classical music. She not only appreciates the sound but understands the patterns and movements.

Can the two ever live together? They get along great. She lets him breathe. She doesn't make fun of his music nor does she try to convert him to European strings.

Insistence to knuckle under is a love killer.

Only fools try to beat each other. Marriage at its best is complimentary, not competitive.

No Need to Compete
Creative breathing is a far cry from competitiveness. She pursues her interest to gain personal fulfillment. Hopefully, he does the same thing. Only fools try to beat each other. Marriage at its best is complimentary and not competitive.

By the time I met one couple, they were well on their way to becoming divorced. They owned a paint and paper store but were not working well together. Finally, he decided to open a similar store in a nearby town, to be managed by his wife. The reasoning was that they could buy in greater volume and business would double.

That was the reasoning on the surface. Each evening their conversations seemed to take an ugly turn. They compared each day's sales with glee and despair. The husband couldn't stand to have his wife outsell him. If a customer complained or returned something, the other partner acted like a gold medal finalist.

Within a few months they decided not to live together any longer.

When both partners have careers, the competition can be terrific. Especially if she is making more money than he. Many husbands are not ready to handle this one yet. But we are beginning to grow up.

Watch yourselves even now when you play games. Do you have to win? Does your partner take it personally if he loses? This could be a good time to talk it over. Little things too often turn into icebergs.

When we first got married, my wife and I played a game of checkers. Not far into the game I made a triple jump. Pat quit immediately. We have played a lot of other games during the past twenty-seven years, but we have yet to play a second game of checkers.

We get along too well to fight over a red and black board. Two strangers are still having the fun of getting to know each other.

Talk It Over

1. When are your low times? What hour of the day are you the dullest? How could you improve that?
2. Do your gifts normally have strings attached?
3. Are you highly competitive? Do you have to win over your partner?
4. Is there something your partner needs to know about you today? What might it be?
5. What is one happy part of your marriage you are looking forward to?

6

A
GREAT
MARRIAGE

A great marriage—that is what your marriage promises to be. One fantastic union.

If we discuss problems too much, we could lose sight of the pleasure. Your marriage has tremendous prospects. It will do you good to stop and recount the great things the two of you have going.

Do you ever wonder why God put marriages together? There are five strong reasons for a good union. If you eventually have all of them going, your relationship will be as healthy as Bruce Jenner with a suntan.

Many partners are extremely happy with only two or three of the five. However, the more of the five you have, the better off you will be. The five are like nails. You can nail a board down with one nail. Through wear and tear the board could break loose after a time. If you have three, four, or five nails, there is less likelihood it will move.

Count your nails. You may have more than five. The more you have, the better.

Nail One
The first nail is the need to complement each other (see Gen. 2:18). In short, it means the two of you are pulling

together rather than apart. Don't make it more complicated than this.

You can marry someone with a similar personalilty or an opposite one. One of you can be the wage earner or you both can work.

In the past we put too much emphasis on the man. We acted as if the woman existed to complement her husband but not the reverse. Now we admit we know better. A male's role in marriage is to complement his wife. Love is supportive, uplifting, and it looks for ways to enhance the person we love (see Eph. 5:25).

If you are engaged, you probably have little difficulty with this. You come together fairly smoothly, like the fingers on a hand. Sometimes a finger gets out of joint, but generally it is a nice fit. You are going to have a great marriage because you do not work against each other.

Nail Two

The second nail is emotional love. The two of you support each other by tenderly caring (see 1 Cor. 13).

You have found someone who listens and tries to understand. When something goes well at work, you can hardly wait to tell her. It means all the more if that person really cares what happens to you. At five o'clock you hurry home with a sheepish grin. Sometimes you blurt it out, other times you play it coy. Once in a while you bring a box of candy.

There is something fantastic to share, and you have a loving partner who will beam at the news.

When part of your world caves in, there is a shoulder at home and a patient ear. This applies not only to the big ups and downs but to everything in between. A new tie and a cut finger. A new car and a leaking roof. This is the emotional love most of us need.

You can see it in high gear while you are engaged. Cultivate it. Keep it fresh.

Nail Three

A third nail is physical love (see 1 Cor. 7:3-5). Sex is a pyramid of strong and varied stones. It is much more than physical release.

Sex is communication. It is a reduction of tension. Sex is simple pleasure. It is a reassurance of belonging.

As an engaged couple, you are moving steadily to its consummation in God's ideal setting—a marriage context. Because your attitudes are healthy, wholesome, and enthusiastic, you will drive this nail deeply.

Nail Four

The fourth nail is children (see Gen. 1:28; Ps. 127:5). Under most conditions, marriage functions as a triangle. Each partner supplies love to the other. They, in turn, pour out their love in a third direction—many times, to children. Then love travels from the third direction back toward the couple.

Children are not necessary for all couples. However, most partners will find parenthood a fulfilling opportunity.

Since both of you have an open attitude toward children, your future looks all the stronger. You can work out the details later.

Adoption will supply this nail just as well as physical birth.

Nail Five

The fifth nail is worship (see Titus 2:5). This is more than worshiping God together. It is more than going to church.

When our marriage is a loving unit, our relationship is itself a worship to God. People will see your love for each other. They will see the stability of your union. God is pleased when he sees this good use of his institution.

A good marriage is a present to God. When he sees two partners madly in love, he is pleased. When he sees children being raised in a wholesome home, he is gratified.

People see a healthy marriage, and they, too, are made happy. If they know that home is Christian, they also receive a favorable witness to the effectiveness of a relationship with Jesus Christ.

Your great marriage is an offering going up to God. It is acceptable and pleasing to him.

Sex is communication. It is a reduction of tension. Sex is simple pleasure. It is a reassurance of belonging.

Rate Your Strengths

These are only five nails. There are probably more. Maybe you can come up with ten. I would encourage you to try. There are definitely five, and because these are part of your plans, your marriage will be especially strong.

Some marriages do not have all five, and the couples are as happy as raccoons at a picnic. Maybe they have decided not to have children. Possibly after some years they have practically given up sex. They have other interests and seldom consider it worth the effort.

Don't assume these marriages are unhappy. They may be getting along excellently on three nails. However, they are the exception. Most couples need every nail they can get. When the wind blows and the rain pours and the house rocks, you will be glad for every nail you have. Your marriage will be fantastic because you will carefully drive each nail firm and straight.

But there are more reasons than this for exhilaration. Take time and recount your strengths and weaknesses as a couple. Be specific. Talk to your partner about this for a few minutes. What will make yours a great marriage? It will help you to write the reasons down.

At first couples are usually too modest to open up, but once they get started, it can flow. This can be a giant step toward feeling reassured about your marriage.

John started out slowly. Finally, he said, "June is so easy to talk to. All day I talk about work or football or even politics. When I see her that evening I can tell her how I really feel. She listens to what is important to me."

Fantastic! It is common strengths that will make this marriage stronger than steel.

Now it's June's turn. "We like to do things together. I've dated other guys, and they always wanted to go places I didn't particularly enjoy. With John it's different."

John comes back. "I enjoy boating and so does June. In good weather we take my boat to the lake."

It isn't that difficult once you get started. We rehearse the problems of marriage. We are flooded with warnings. It is more important to remember all those outstanding qualities you two have going for you.

Take another productive step. Share with your partner

what you like best about him or her. Why in the world do you love him? Love has reasons.

One young man told me, "Colleen isn't too smart and neither am I, so I figure we will get along great."

Sound the alarm. Abandon ship. What a miserable foundation for a marriage!

By reminding your partner of the features you like most, you reinforce them. Years ago my wife said she really appreciated the way I pick up my own clothes. To this day it haunts me. Every time I start to leave socks on the floor, her compliment echoes in my brain. By pointing out a strength, she made it stronger.

You can do this dozens of times. Do you think she is a neat dresser? Tell her so, and you might seal it forever. Do you like her trim figure? Say so, and she is more likely to keep it. Say you like her few extra pounds, and it will probably have the same effect. Do you like the way he drives the car? Nail it down before it gets away.

Is he saying please and thank you? Tell him he is one of the most courteous people you know. He'll eat it up.

What do you like to do together? Be specific. Do you go skating, hiking, bowling? Do you like to listen to music, play games, work in the church? This will help you see what a wide base of interests you share. If it's only one or two, you will want to work at expanding the list. Some marriages suffer from too few interests.

What are your emotional strengths? Pam said, "We get along great until Rich has a problem. Then he clams up and won't talk. He isn't mean, but I wish he would say something."

A *good marriage is a present to God. When he sees two partners madly in love, he is pleased. When he sees children being raised in a wholesome home, he is gratified.*

Chart Your Dreams
Once you start building and reinforcing each other, ask yourselves what your hopes are as a couple. How do you picture yourselves ten years from now? Dream out loud.

Where will your career be? This is not just a question for professional people but for all with careers. It is a question for both men and women. Does she plan to work? How long? Does she dream of being the manager of a savings and loan? Discuss it now and begin to mesh your dreams together.

Is there a special place you would like to live a few years from now? Do you plan to buy a home? What kind? How will you go about getting a down payment or financing? It's all hope material.

Discussing dreams openly helps make your sights realistic. It also helps to keep you both on the same track.

Check Your Growth

You don't want to have a stroke every time you get a hangnail, but neither do you want to go into a trance. Solid sharing often does not come easily. While you are engaged, practice working out your emotions in a balanced way.

Some people always demand attention. They think what they have to say is most important. In their opinion, everything should stop immediately. They interrupt conversations, activities, even phone calls. Listen to what I have to say, they seem to shout.

One of my children did this constantly. She was only eight at the time. Today she still likes to share, but she has more self-control.

We may not always be able to control our emotions, but we can work at improving this ability. Look at the ways you are progressing emotionally. It's a good sign. You feel more comfortable together. Are you managing depression better? Is discouragement becoming less habitual? You are leveling off to a solid, livable pace.

How do you rate your ability to change? If you are becoming more like your partner, don't despair. In most cases this is excellent. If your partner is also becoming like you, the situation is ideal.

Be glad you are not cemented. If one of you were standing still, you would have reason for concern. Some partners believe the aim of marriage is for the other partner to conform. Such a person is like a park statue. He never changes himself, except to discolor.

If you can name some positive changes you have made because of your partner, your relationship is throbbing. Keep on exercising. Your goal is not identical twins but compatibility.

Check out your mind growth, too. It is an excellent sign to see you reading this book. It is an excellent sign to know you read any books. Relationships can grow from fresh and stimulating ideas—not just about marriage but on practically any subject.

Read the paper, watch the news. You can share and grow by the injection of new material.

Discuss Your Differences

While you are discussing good questions, throw this one on the fire: How would you like to improve your partner? Here's a good chance to make progress.

Have you wanted him to give up smoking? Do both of you a favor and let him know now. Most partners are patient and pliable this close to marriage. Be frank but kind.

One partner answered this question by saying, "My only wish is that Dave would quit drinking. He doesn't drink much, but I couldn't stand to have it in our house."

We discussed her feelings. Dave had never been drunk and found it hard to understand why she felt so strongly. They could resolve their difference far easier now than they might after marriage. In this case, it was no big deal with Dave, and the drinking was gone.

Often the suggestions are appreciated. Your partner knows you really love him and only have his interest at heart.

Turn the question around. How can you improve yourself to best help your marriage? There is no need for excessive introspection. Just a quick survey should come up with a couple of winners.

A few solid sacrifices for your partner will be a terrific investment in your marriage. Volunteer without being asked.

You know she thinks the radio is too loud in the car. Next time have it on low and surprise her. She never will get used to your sardines and onions. Switch to tuna fish.

Don't feel like a martyr. It is all part of putting a stable marriage together. And yours really will be a great one.

How do you picture yourselves ten years from now? Dream out loud.

Talk It Over

1. Which three nails of the five nails mentioned in the chapter do you feel are strongest in your relationship?
2. Can you name one nail your marriage will have that is not mentioned in the five?
3. In two sentences explain why yours will be a great marriage.

7

THE "HIDDEN" PROBLEM

SANDRA and Mike were one of the nicest couples you could hope to meet. They had known each other for eighteen months and had been engaged for six. You could tell they were in love, not because they pored over each other but because both glowed like warm ovens.

One of the questions I try to ask a couple is, "How would you change your partner?" After some polite denials, most of them come across with helpful suggestions.

Mike finally pushed it out slowly, like toothpaste.

"I wish she wasn't so jealous."

"How is Sandra jealous, Mike?" I asked.

"If she sees me even wave at a girl, she won't talk to me. I'm afraid after we are married, I won't have any old friends."

"Why?" I wanted to know.

After some discussion, the facts became obvious to all three of us. Sandra felt she had nothing to offer. She didn't consider herself attractive or capable and thought she was barely likable. Consequently, every situation was a threat to her.

Sandra represents millions of people who have little

respect for themselves. Their inability to love themselves can place great strain on their marriage.

The Best Gift You Can Give

If you can give your partner only one present, make it a healthy respect for yourself. It is much easier to love someone who has a healthy love for himself or herself.

For years I counseled husbands and wives who had "little" problems. They complained about money, sex, and communication. One day after a frustrating session, I sat back bewildered. For an hour I had discussed a silly situation with a young married woman. Finally, we applied a bandage and she left with a sense of relief. But it was only one of many problems she had. Then it dawned on me. This woman had so little respect for herself that she would always be swamped with small problems. If she was ever to level off, she needed to adopt a healthy attitude toward herself.

Everyone should meet Erv. He would do anything for you—and not just if you asked him. He would look for ways to help, regardless. Erv loved himself. He took flying lessons, went to graduate school part-time, went hunting, sang in a quartet. He was the busiest person you could imagine, yet he was the most unselfish man. Self-love and selfishness do not have to be the same thing.

If we don't consider ourselves lovable, we will make it tough on our partners.

Deep inside, most of us probably do love ourselves. Many of us are embarrassed by it. We don't know how to handle it. Often we have been taught it is wrong. We spend much of our lives trying to smother it. Now we need to accept a balanced concept. The Bible tells us it is OK to love ourselves because it leads to a love for others (see Eph. 5:33).

"My husband doesn't love me." The woman speaking was a young, attractive redhead with despair in her voice. "I didn't believe he loved me when we were going together, and after three years of marriage, I still don't believe it."

Her cry for help was the same one raised by thousands of other married people. Her husband was considerate, thoughtful, and careful to tell her how much he loved her. Still, something inside kept telling her he didn't. She simply didn't believe she was worthy of being loved.

The apostle Paul understood this principle. He wrote to tell husbands to love their wives as they love themselves (see Eph. 5:28).

Before you stand at the altar, do your partner a gigantic favor. Sit down and make a list of all the things you do well—little things you never think of, big things you do all the time. Don't stop until you have ten. If you can give twenty, you are really sailing.

Some will find this hard to do. A few will never get it done. But make an attempt to look at yourself realistically rather than surrendering to the great put-down.

Do anything you care to with the note. Maybe you will want to give it to your partner and explain it. Possibly you will want to trade lists. Whether your mate ever sees it or not isn't what counts. The fact that you made it will be the greatest wedding present you could give.

Maybe your list will start off with some of these:

1. *Listen well*
2. *Like to help*
3. *Good friend*
4. *Patient*
5. *Complimentary*
6. *Allow freedom to others*

These are genuine strengths that you most likely have even if you have trouble accepting them.

Taking Care

Not only do you need a good opinion of yourself, but you need to keep it. Many couples start their marriage feeling great and soon go under. With children to feed, floors to scrub, and a career to pursue, it is easy to come apart. Our marriages can't afford that.

A number of years ago there was a commercial on television advertising a tonic. A married couple look at each other and say, "We take good care of ourselves." I don't know if the product works. I do know the principle is sound.

Fatigue and pressure are termites to any marriage.

If you can give your partner only one present, make it a healthy respect for yourself.

They will destroy your concept of yourself. Promise yourself you will help your marriage by keeping yourself in good condition physically, mentally, and spiritually.

A Hidden Problem

The way we feel about ourselves is contagious. Our feelings of uselessness will eventually affect our mate, both directly and indirectly. If we consider ourselves worthless, we will pass it on to our children.

Paul taught that a man should accept his wife as part of his body and give her the same love and care he would give himself (see Eph. 5:28). A sane man does not cut off his hand or intentionally run a tractor over his foot.

If a person considers himself unworthy, useless, or friendless, he may transfer that feeling to his wife. His thinking may go something like this: I do not deserve good food; consequently, we do not deserve good food. I do not like having friends over; consequently, we do not have friends over. I am not capable of being a leader; therefore, I am embarrassed when my wife leads.

Ephesians 5:28 spells out what is essential to a balanced marriage. Take a happy, healthy attitude toward your spouse in the same way you take a happy, healthy attitude toward yourself.

A wife complains to a counselor: "He never talks to me. He won't give me his opinion or take any leadership. What am I supposed to do?" That problem gets listed as communication breakdown. In reality, the husband is unsure of himself, does not think his opinion is worthwhile, and would rather remain silent than sound foolish. He actually has a problem of feeling low self-worth. The refusal to communicate is only the symptom of the difficulty and not the cause.

Jane was in her mid-twenties and had been married for five years. She found it impossible to enjoy sex.

"I wish he would leave me alone. It just gives me the creeps to know he is coming after me. In the daytime everything is fine, but I dread nighttime."

It sounds like a classic sex problem. Where is the root cause? Is he an offensive or clumsy lover? Maybe she had a bad experience in her youth.

After talking to Jane for two sessions, the difficulty became apparent to both of us. She thought of herself as ugly. She couldn't imagine anyone wanting to make love to her. Her entire body would go frigid just to think of the encounter. Rather than flooding her with sex literature, we began to deal with the hidden problem.

Couples who are deeply in love could be heading for critical conflicts without understanding the reason. We need to back off and ask crucial questions about our self-respect.

Five Truths about You

Fortunately, help is available for just such a difficulty. We need to accept some simple but startling facts about ourselves. Here are some things we need to tell ourselves and rehearse often.

1. *I am a valuable person.* Sometimes, standing nose deep in self-pity, we tell ourselves we don't amount to anything. We consider ourselves Mr. Zeros, the dandruff of the world.

This false modesty sounds pious among Christians. However, the Bible won't let us get away with it. God created us in his image (see Gen. 1:27). As we know, people fell into sin and lost some of that image (see Rom. 5:12). But if this is all we know, we have heard only part of the good news. Jesus Christ picked us up, dusted us off, and reunited us with God (see Col. 1:21-22).

No longer ding-a-lings, people have a purpose and plan in life. God considers us valuable, and he wants us to participate in his program in this world.

A despondent wife sits on the sofa engulfed in a cloud of gloom. She feels useless. She is not any good. Her children would be better off without her. We can combat this scene by placing some simple facts in order and keeping them there.

2. *I am capable.* It is difficult for many people to admit they can do anything. I have asked individuals to make a list of ten things they do well. They have agonized, sweated, and strained over it. Finally they came back and said, "Forget it." They simply couldn't force themselves to do it.

Promise yourself you will help your marriage by keeping yourself in good condition physically, mentally, and spiritually.

To say we are capable sounds like pride, conceit, and all those other nasty things. For many, it is a mental hurdle they cannot leap.

In the marriage relationship, this feeling burns like the hot sun through a glass. A husband hates to fix anything, so his wife assumes he is lazy. Quite the contrary; he thinks he is incapable of fixing anything. She doesn't want to try anything new. He thinks she is an old-fashioned stick-in-the-mud. The fact is, she doesn't think she can do anything new or she will fail.

Romans 12:3-8 tells us to not think of ourselves more highly than we ought. It seems everyone knows that part. What many fail to realize is that this passage goes on to say that people should have a sober judgment or face the facts. The facts are that believers have gifts given to them by God that they need to recognize and use. To feel you can do nothing is a denial of reality.

You are a gifted person. I don't have to know you or give you a battery of tests. The fact that you are a person means you are gifted. Celebrate that giftedness rather than deny it.

3. *I am loved.* A baseball player for the Kansas City Royals got into a fight with New York Yankee players. A reporter later said to him, "You know the Yankees are really mad at you." He replied, "I have a wife and two children who love me. I don't need to have the Yankees love me, too."

Great wisdom! Too many people want everyone to love them. Because not everyone loves them, they assume no one does. A case of tragic extremes.

"I was married five years before I believed she loved me." That is a sad statement because the husband's feelings have robbed him of a great deal of happiness. However, this is not an uncommon feeling. Yet this is usually all it is—just a feeling.

Do your mate a huge favor. Resolve for yourself once and for all that your partner loves you. Otherwise you will find it difficult to relax and give yourself to your spouse.

It is amazing how many people do not believe anyone loves them. Some Christians do not believe God loves them. Children do not believe their parents love them. Some people believe their spouse doesn't care.

Rather than accepting true love, which rises above circumstances, they continue to play an immature game called "Nobody loves me." The result is a very self-centered life. "Where will I find love?" "Is he mad at me?" "She wishes she had never married me."

Some terribly rude things can be said between a husband and wife. A partner often becomes less careful or courteous after the honeymoon. While dating, a couple is always kind and loving. But after months or years of familiarity, it becomes easy to be thoughtlessly frank. "Those slacks look crummy." "Didn't we eat this last night?" "You are always watching football." Sometimes these phrases, thrown around loosely, can cut deeply. They might lead you to wonder if you are really loved.

True love is not a magic act—now you see it, now you don't. Drive this nail firmly into your marriage and you can depend on it. A few thoughtless statements and careless actions cannot erase your love for each other. You are loved. You can count on it.

Because some people are always seeking love and never finding it, they have trouble leading balanced lives. They find it difficult to relax and even more difficult to help others.

You are correct. You are not the most loved person in the world. Neither are you the most hated. You are you. You have someone who is willing to spend the rest of his life with you. You are greatly loved.

Certainly God doesn't love his children with a fickle love. Jeremiah said, "For long ago the Lord had said to Israel: I have loved you, O my people, with an everlasting love; with loving-kindness I have drawn you to me" (Jer. 31:3).

God's love is constant and unchanging. Most of us will have a mate who is basically the same way. Some only imagine their spouses change like a kaleidoscope with each flick of the wrist. Most likely, a partner has contributed plenty to prove his love. The next time he says it, you should just believe it.

4. *I am improving*. "We have been married for fifteen

The fact that you are a person means you are gifted. Celebrate that giftedness rather than deny it.

years, and we love each other more today that we did then."

Do you ever wonder how many say this and don't really mean it? I think some are just pretending. They have to say something, and they can't say, "This marriage is lousy." Yet others say it with a deep and warm conviction.

What is the difference between the sincere ones and the pretenders? Which one will you be a dozen years from now? Just possibly what makes the difference is whether you choose to grow and improve during your years together.

"I wouldn't go back to dating for anything." The man who said this had been married for years. "The uncertainty, the anxiety—it seemed like fun then, but it doesn't rate compared to the dependability of marriage."

Now they know, they share, they trust, they confide much more than they ever did before. They have matured and accept each other more. Their life together really is richer than it was when they first married.

Many people have trouble finding the comfortable middle in life. They wrestle continuously between inferiority and superiority. Today he thinks he is the greatest, and his ego lifts like steam whistling from a kettle. The next day he is the world's worst and tries to join the night crawlers under a damp rock.

After years of war within yourself, you finally admit the facts. "I am not inferior. I am not superior. I am me." You have grown and improved, and your family will be the better for it.

But this shouldn't surprise us. Paul wrote, "I am sure that God who began the good work within you will keep right on helping you grow in his grace until his task within you is finally finished on that day when Jesus Christ returns" (Phil. 1:6).

Does this promise apply just to missionaries or new Christians? It applies to people, and people make up marriages. Because people are improving, your marriage will improve also.

If God wills you to live tomorrow, you can improve, and both partners can thank God for that.

5. *It is reasonable to love myself.* Most men are not the best husbands in the world, but neither are they the

worst. They are just good husbands. They will look back at terrible blunders they made. Sometimes they really embarrassed their wives. Many husbands will also remember the things they did that brought the broadest smile and brightest sparkle ever to light up a wife.

There are many times husbands or wives have done the job well. It would do them good to admit it to themselves. It will even encourage them to do well the next time.

I find it easier to emphasize the negative. I can remember failures in vivid, living color. It would be hard to forget them since I tend to recite them over and over. A few years ago, I took a step toward combating this negativism. Now I collect and keep every compliment I get. If I get a thank-you note or letter, I no longer throw it away. I keep it in a special drawer. Every once in a while, I take out all the notes and go over them. It's a great morale builder.

I look at those notes and say to myself, "Yes, I did that. This was fun. I'm proud of that job." Sometimes it helps keep me in balance.

Rehearse the things you do well. It can help you do even better next time.

God reminds us it is good to have a healthy respect for ourselves. It is out of this health that we will best be able to love others, especially our partners.

"That is how husbands should treat their wives, loving them as parts of themselves. For since a man and his wife are now one, a man is really doing himself a favor and loving himself when he loves his wife" (Eph. 5:28).

If self-love, self-respect, and self-worth can all be handled in correct proportion, the net result is freedom. Freedom for yourself, your partner, and, eventually, your family. It is all right if your husband goes hunting because you like to go bowling. And your husband is free to pursue a career because you have some goals you want to accomplish.

The two of you are not jealous—you are not in competition. Consequently, you are not afraid to let go. You realize you can better keep someone by giving him freedom.

Some fathers or mothers have smothered their families.

Too many people want everyone to love them. Because not everyone loves them, they assume no one does.

They wanted everyone close each evening. They insisted the household revolve around them. Often they were trying to create a love they did not have for themselves.

You are free. Free to commit yourselves to each other. Not because your partner demands allegiance but because you want to give it. Because you are happy with yourself, you are not afraid to give yourself to someone else.

Talk It Over
1. How does your partner put himself or herself down? How could you help change that practice?
2. Are you able to accept the fact that your partner loves you? If not, what would it take to convince you?
3. How is God changing your life presently?

8

SEXUAL LIMBO

ENGAGEMENT is the stage of enormous sexual frustration and hope. The two of you want each other. Nothing could be more natural. If you have no sex drive, there is reason to see a doctor. If you don't find each other appealing, you might as well call it off.

The feelings you have are healthy and God-given. If we weren't sex magnets, the population would soon dwindle. We would also miss a great deal of happiness.

Now that you are promised to each other, the desire will probably intensify. Congratulations! Everything is going according to schedule.

The problem is, you sort of "half" own each other. You fully intend to marry. Only weeks or months stand between you and sexual fulfillment. The question now is whether you will hold off until marriage and enjoy sex in its fullest freedom.

Why Wait?
Statistics tell us many couples are participating in premarital, extramarital, and nonmarital sex. Television seems to be promoting sex outside of a marriage context. Most situation comedies feature characters who are not married.

Does it make any sense for a young couple to wait until they are married? Our society is increasingly tolerant of premarital sex. It is often treated as not only acceptable but cute.

Frankly, engaged couples can do what they want today. If they are adult enough to marry, they should be mature enough to intelligently decide about their sex life. However, the fact that they have this freedom doesn't mean they have to use it.

I am free to bake in the sun for hours and burn like bacon. But I don't have to do it to prove I am free. I am at liberty to throw my money down a sewer grate—another freedom I choose to ignore.

Anyone who chooses premarital sex and doesn't care about the consequences probably isn't mature enough to marry.

With so many opinions and practices being freely publicized, young people will have to make up their own minds. Whose system of ethics and conduct are they willing to accept?

Fortunately, the Bible offers direct guidance on the subject. It is a book of understanding and practical instruction. God knows how you feel right now. He appreciates your dreams, hopes, desires, and frustrations.

Knowing exactly what we are going through, God tells us to stay away from premarital intercourse. "That is why I say to run from sex sin. No other sin affects the body as this one does. When you sin this sin it is against your own body" (1 Cor. 6:18).

Jesus Christ reminded us that physical union is marriage union. "The two shall become one—no longer two, but one! And no man may divorce what God has joined together" (Matt. 19:6).

Sexual fads and practices come and go. One day it is popular, even fashionable, to entertain sexual adventures. Trial marriages and living together become daring. However, tomorrow the wind shifts, and we are off chasing the next illusion.

We need a dependable guideline. God unflinchingly offers us one.

In our enlightened age, we might think the traditional

warnings are no longer necessary. With birth control measures the risk of pregnancy should be diminished. With massive education the threat of venereal disease should be eliminated. Yet in some American cities, the number of abortions exceeds the number of regular births. VD is at an all-time high, and AIDS has crossed into the heterosexual community.*

These facts seem almost too obvious to mention. They sound like old scare tactics that won't work in a modern society. Yet it is embarrassing to see how widespread the consequences are. Premarital sex remains both physically unsafe and unwise.

We are suspicious that these are not the ultimate reasons for God's warning. They are important, but they are only by-products. The essential reason for waiting has to do with the marriage relationship.

Sex is a special form of communication you save for one person. It comforts, relaxes, reassures, and sometimes makes you want to shout. It is reserved by both the male and female for one person who needs the ultimate communication. God considers this gift too majestic to share indiscriminately.

Smart partners will make up their minds early. There are many couples who wish they had waited until marriage. *I have never met a Christian couple that was sorry they waited.*

Sex is a special form of communication you save for one person. . . . God considers this gift too majestic to share indiscriminately.

After Your Decision
When you have made your commitment to wait, there are several steps you need to consider. They are practical and unspectacular. You can add suggestions of your own.

Couples need to avoid bumming around. After they have gone together for a while, it becomes easier to sit around and do nothing in particular. Often these nothing dates degenerate quickly. Young people begin to kiss or pet, partly out of boredom. Frankly, they have nothing

*If a blood test is not required in your state, be sure and get one anyway. Even if AIDS is not a question in your relationship, be sure there are as few surprises as possible. Couples need to enter marriage with the best knowledge they can get. Maybe your blood types need to be discussed, or one of you might have a condition that can be treated early.

else to do with their hands. There is no plan to get heavy, but there is really nothing better to do. Couples may find themselves far more involved than they expected to be.

It is important to plan your evening. Develop some mutual interests and activities. These will prove beneficial when you are married.

A wise person once told a group of young people to "get out of those cars." They laughed at him. How prudish can you be? When they grew up, they told their children, "Get out of those cars." Their children laughed at them.

And so the generations go. Two people parking in a car are a certain invitation for sexual adventure. All of us know it is true. When you are young, you hate to admit it.

The person who really wants to avoid premarital intercourse will stay away from places where it is likely to happen. If you want to save money, you stay out of stores. When you want to wait until marriage, you avoid traps.

Certain movies put intense pressure on couples. You have the right to attend. However, only the foolish think they can handle everything.

No engaged couple can afford to ignore Hamburg's law. Briefly stated, it says a couple never regresses physically. If a couple kisses, they will kiss again. If they fondle, they will fondle again. If they have intercourse, they will have it again.

The partners who say, "Let's do it just once," are kidding themselves. Couples do not regress in physical love. They either repeat or progress. They seldom quit.

Maybe you are the exception. Most people think they are. They find out too late they are not. Guard your physical progress, or it will soon get out of control.

It is easy to see why a young person is in a physical "rush." He has rounded the corner of twenty and by now has survived strong sexual pressure. Magazines, literature, jokes, films have all painted the real and the supposed glories of sex. His own body has ached for sexual release. How much longer does he have to wait? He has found the person he wants to marry. Both partners imagine that sexual adventure can only strengthen their relationship.

Don't let your physical needs fog your brain. Intercourse will only complicate your needs rather than ease your tension. Surveys indicate a third to a half of all engagements break up. Your marriage plans may not be as definite as you hope. Frequently, the frustrations accompanying premarital sex lead to an eventual split.

Many young people argue late into the night over how much difference a piece of paper makes. If they are married in their hearts, can't they also be married with their bodies?

It is true that the biblical definition of marriage is two people joining in sexual love. Isaac is a good example. He married Rebekah by taking her to his tent (see Gen. 24:67). Jacob evidently married Rachel by sleeping with her (see Gen. 29:30). Two people became one flesh.

However, God has given government the right to regulate marriage. If the law asks for a certificate, a Christian is happy to comply. Even if laws should change, Christian marriage will remain a total commitment.

Arguments against the government's rights are mere contortions. They are irrational attempts to sidestep the law in order to surrender to lust.

When a couple starts to give in to this illogic, they need to stop and ask themselves some questions. Just what is the hurry? Why not get a piece of paper? Is this an indication of the impetuous behavior that will mark your marriage? Are you sure both of you are mature enough to handle these important decisions? Just being in a hurry is no sign you are ready to marry.

Marriage is filled with little surprises. You will want to start it with the most solid foundation possible. God understands what's best for us, and obedience does pay off. Patience will pay large dividends later.

"But let patience have her perfect work, that ye may be perfect and entire, wanting nothing" (James 1:4, KJV).

Surveys indicate that couples who live together evidence a higher rate of marital discord and divorce than those who are married.

Rumors about Sex

As you put a Christian standard to work, you must erase certain myths. Much nonsense being passed around today has no basis in fact.

For instance, the rumor that everyone is doing it is a complete fairy tale. It is the same story that passed around a generation ago. Many couples do participate in premarital intercourse. But millions do not. And yet they could if they wanted. Movies are particularly devastating in distorting the facts. They often make it appear that every couple is involved in sex. This is far from the case, even among college students.

Yet it is an argument that is hard to dismiss. When we get the feeling "everyone" does it, we begin to wonder about ourselves. Are we weird because we haven't? Is there something terrific in youth I might miss? Consequently, the pressure becomes tremendous.

It takes a particularly secure person to resist in the light of these trends. The "pack" person falls easily to this argument. The thinker will stop and decide for himself. The Christian knows there are more important things to consider than trends or surveys.

Another myth that needs exposure is the trial marriage approach. Two are supposed to have sex to see if they are physically compatible. Possibly they won't enjoy each other in bed. Is it better to find out now?

As plausible as this sounds to some, the facts prove the opposite. In their surveys, Dr. Judson Landis and Dr. Evelyn Duvall both found evidence that premarital sex is unprofitable. Most women seldom experienced sexual climax with intercourse before marriage. However, the frequency rose considerably after the two adapted during marriage.

Living together sounds appealing to many young couples, and it's true that a considerable number are trying it. But keep this in mind: Surveys indicate that couples who live together evidence a higher rate of marital discord and divorce than those who are married. Studies in Sweden have found the divorce rate among those who lived together before marriage to be significantly higher than those who did not. A University of Nebraska study concluded that there is a "modest but consistent relationship between cohabitation and lower marital interaction, elevated disagreement, divorce proneness, and divorce and permanent separation among nonminorities."

Neither study suggests that premarital cohabitation causes divorce in marriage. It may well be that people with nonconventional life-styles and defiance for authority are more likely to live together; consequently, they are more likely to defy accepted norms and divorce. However, that does not change the dangers of living together. If you and your partner have a low regard for the sanctity of marriage before the wedding, you are more likely to have a low regard of marriage if you ever consider divorce.

There seems to be no good way to "practice" being married. An essential key to marriage is commitment. There is no way to be tentatively committed. The University of Nebraska survey found *no* support for the theory that premarital cohabitation is a good training ground for marriage or that it improved mate selection.

Before marriage the couple has sex without commitment. Tomorrow the relationship could end. They hold a promise to each other, but both realize it is not binding. Should they fail to enjoy this relationship, they could merely elect to split.

There is no such thing as laboratory marriage. We are not white mice. There can be no experiments in this field. Two people cannot pretend to care and have total commitment and get the same result.

The smart couple will learn a number of things about each other before marriage. Sex performance and compatibility are not among them. Most married couples adapt and improve their sex experience because they are dedicated to success, not because they are experimenting.

An essential key to marriage is commitment. There is no way to be tentatively committed.

Proof of Love

Too many couples are still engaging in premarital sex to "prove" they love their partner. That line is as old as stone. Before you fall into this pattern, face some facts.

The partner who demands sex as proof of love is flatly exploitative. He is looking out for himself at your expense. How you feel about it is not his primary concern. He has an ego to satisfy. It is much like deer hunting, and you are the deer. He needs to score in order to please himself. If a partner continues to act this way, he is sending a clear message. The individual is extremely selfish and generally is looking out for himself. He doesn't care that you might be used or your feelings may be hurt.

Do yourself a favor and think this person over. The

rest of your life may be spent as the servant of a tireless tyrant. At least you need to discuss this matter and reach some understanding.

On the other hand, what type of person feels the need to give in to such selfishness? If you want to wait until marriage but give in beforehand, what kind of strength are you showing? If you feel so insecure that you cannot hold your ground, how will you fare after your marriage? Can it survive with one dominant figure demanding your compliance?

Of course, you think, it will be different when you get married. The two of you won't have these frustrations, and you can join in gladly. Don't kid yourself. The patterns you set in engagement are often the same ones that linger through a lifetime.

God is far from being opposed to sex. He only wants it practiced under healthy control. This is why he made it a pleasure rather than a pain. Far from being against it, God is the promoter of married sex (see 1 Cor. 7:1-5).

There are good reasons for lines down the middle of highways. Waterways may be open, but careful laws keep them safe.

"If a godly man compromises with the wicked, it is like polluting a fountain or muddying a spring" (Prov. 25:26).

Forgiveness
Despite the strong teaching of the Scriptures, there are many who have had premarital intercourse. Unfortunately, too many of these never feel forgiven and free from their sin. However, the Bible not only warns against premarital intercourse and other sins but promises forgiveness, grace, and full restoration for those who repent.

He never bears a grudge, nor remains angry forever.
He has not punished us as we deserve for all our sins,
for his mercy toward those who fear and honor him
is as great as the height of the heavens above the earth.
He has removed our sins as far away from us as the
east is from the west. He is like a father to us, tender

and sympathetic to those who reverence him (Ps. 103:9-13).

Have you already had premarital intercourse? There is no need to continue to drag your guilt around. God promises to forgive those who in true repentance ask his forgiveness.

The person who has had sex before marriage is wrong. God doesn't equivocate. But it would be hypocritical for the rest of us to judge that person harshly. "Yes, all have sinned; all fall short of God's glorious ideal; yet now God declares us 'not guilty' of offending him if we trust in Jesus Christ, who in his kindness freely takes away our sins" (Rom. 3:23).

No matter how far you go physically, the engagement period is trying. You love the person you are committed to. The person is attractive, appealing, and interesting. Marriage will mean the two of you will sleep together and enjoy sex. You can't be considered odd if you want to hurry that up.

If you have had intercourse, don't think the marriage can't work. Thousands of couples who have had premarital sex go on to highly successful marriages. However, many of them need to take time to deal with what has happened. They are better off because they have aired it and cleared their feelings. Ultimate healing is possible only because of genuine repentance, confession to God, and restoration.

Communicate with each other during the engagement period. Tell your partner how you feel about sex. Then plan together what you can do to keep it in bounds until the right time comes.

Talk It Over
1. Do you and your partner find yourselves in some high-risk situations? What can you change to help safeguard yourselves from sexual activity?
2. Is there a sexual situation for which you need to apologize and forgive each other? Have you done that?

If you have had intercourse, don't think the marriage can't work.

9

LOVE COMMUNICATES

WHEN she put on her shoe, her toes felt funny. She reached inside and found a piece of white paper. Written in red ink were the simple words: "I love you today." It wasn't signed—and it didn't have to be. She had the greatest husband in the world. For the rest of the day, the young lady's battery would be charged. Her husband had communicated without saying a word out loud.

Most engaged couples seem to find it easy to communicate. They have so much to talk about. There are plans to make, futures to dream, and new frontiers to explore in each other's personality.

There are not only reasons to communicate but also many avenues for communication. An engaged couple can look into each other's eyes and talk for fifteen minutes without saying a word. His hand placed on hers says more than hours of conversation.

The key to a lasting love is to keep it this way. The smart couple will have open, flowing lines of communication to make it easy to say all the things that need to be said.

Don't Forget the Little Things

Barbara and Don used to go for long walks before they were married. But after the rings were put in place, life had a way of becoming complicated. He had to finish graduate school, and then, of course, there was the career he had to develop. Soon their life started to pull apart rather than melt together.

In the process, they forgot the little things. They were too busy to take walks anymore. Everything was hurried, and fast cars were the only way to move. They were too busy to sit and drink from each other's eyes. Love itself had to be hurried and hectic.

Married life doesn't have to be this way. A happy couple can take the communication they have as engaged people and build on it. Don't give up the little things you have now, but keep adding new and exciting avenues.

To some of us the word *communication* sounds so official and heavy, like a summit conference. If things are going badly or something drastic is about to happen, we had better stop and communicate. Maybe we had best make an appointment.

There are some summits in marriage, but not many. There are fewer official conversations for those who keep in touch along the way.

When we were engaged, it was hard to imagine we would ever stop talking. When we walked around Washington, D.C., sat in little restaurants, or called each other, there was so much to say. It was all new, interesting, and exciting.

In married life, it becomes easy to hide behind a newspaper or dissolve into work. It is sometimes a long time before something new happens. We have discussed each other's relatives several times, and there is little new to say. Some family counselors say 80 percent of those who come to see them have this complaint: "We can't seem to talk to each other."

One day I was standing in my kitchen with a friend. He picked up a note off the table and read it. The note said, "You are a great lover. Pat." My friend looked at me, smiled the world's most devilish grin, and said, "It must be nice!"

I was embarrassed. But he was right! It was nice. Some of the best advice I received before marriage came from a patent lawyer. He said, "After you get married, keep doing the little things." Instead of buying the big gift once a year, why not a long-stemmed rose every couple of weeks? Instead of the six-dollar box of candy, try one for fifty-nine cents. The little frequent reminders are the things that turn a heart to putty.

A middle-aged man once explained why he called his wife every night when he was on the road. His first wife had died and it had devastated his heart. Never again could he take his wife for granted. Every night he was determined to communicate just a little.

Accept Your Differences

"She never says anything" was Russell's complaint. "I'm the kind of guy who enjoys talking—but it really gets to me when she just hangs on."

Not an uncommon statement. Sometimes the girl is the talker and the guy is Calvin Coolidge. It would be surprising to find a husband and wife who both enjoyed talking and listening in exact proportion.

After all, marriage is an adjustment. A happy adjustment, hopefully, but an adjustment nevertheless. Both partners need to move toward the center. Russell needs to talk less, and his wife needs to talk more. That is no problem. The problem arises when one partner assumes that his rate of communication is the ideal. Then he can't understand why his mate doesn't become like him. That attitude is trouble.

This is part of the reason why sex is so important. It is not only that there is need for physical release and that sex is fun (and that it is). Rather, if sex had no other function, it is a great help in simple communication.

Sex in a married context says, "I love you." It says someone cares. When things get cold and harsh outside, close, warm physical contact is a message. Sex is love at a high plateau when it indicates someone cares.

Avoid Extremes

Whatever the form of communication, it has to avoid extremes. On the one end are the door crashers. At the other end are the silent nodders.

The door crasher is the impatient type. He wants to

Forcing issues too hard and fast just might cause them to break.

talk about everything *right now*. "Let's get it out in the open" is his motto.

He has a dangerous attitude. Some things need to settle. They need time to mellow and age. Often these will take care of themselves.

Forcing issues too hard and fast just might cause them to break. The sensitive mate learns to read his partner. He knows when to rush in and when to wait in the wings.

Sometimes we get hurt and are hurt learning the difference. But it's worth it to find out.

Speak Up

Smiling nodders are just as bad. They don't feel the need to say anything. They merely grin and assume everything will be all right. Nonsense. No one—absolutely no one—likes to be taken for granted. Anyone who only needs a silent grinner could have married Mount Rushmore.

Pry yourself loose. Make yourself communicate. If it is small, that may be just the touch. Somehow the message that you care must get across in easy-to-understand terms.

Most communication isn't by the words we say. Experts in the field tell us only 7 percent of communication is by words. Inflection and tone make up 38 percent. Facial expression delivers the other 55 percent.

If you doubt this, try an experiment. Practice saying, "Honey, you can do it any way you like." Say it gleefully. Try it scornfully. Say it defiantly. Give it your angry look and tone. Put it in a tender tone.

Words don't mean much. After a big fight, someone will say, "Well, I don't understand. I told him he could go ahead." The important thing is how you told him he could go ahead. You know what it is like to be told you can do something but hear by the tone that you don't dare.

It is hard to overstate the influence we have over our partner. When the two of you meet at the end of a day, that first greeting is terrifically important. "How did the day go, honey?" "The pits" is the acid reply. Those two words have set the tenor for the evening.

She would have been better off to have said something good about the day. A sad face, a grin, a wink can all make the difference.

A man came home one evening after a terrible day. There was no other way to describe it. He piled out of the car with stooped shoulders and a face like a bulldog. Suddenly, he stopped himself. *I can't take this inside,* he thought. He had three children and a hardworking wife. If he crawled inside, the entire atmosphere of the house would drop like a rock. He straightened himself, forced a smile, and marched inside like a conquering hero.

We owe it to the person we love to try and stay on top. *You* are the biggest influence in his or her daily life. Not the only one—just the biggest.

A junior high counselor told me about some role modeling he does in class. He pairs off couples and asks them to pretend they are parents. Almost always they are gruff, loud—practically violent. Seldom are they polite, caring, or affectionate.

No one—absolutely no one—likes to be taken for granted.

Hold Your Tongue

Before we go too far with our emphasis on communication, one rule should be kept in mind. Some things aren't worth saying. A man may say, "I can say anything I want to my wife." Shame on him.

The Bible says, "A man with good sense holds his tongue" (Prov. 11:12). Everyone needs a filter between his brain and his tongue. We think many things we shouldn't say. We think many things we shouldn't even think.

There is a point at which frankness becomes ugly. The person who always shoots off how he thinks is dangerous. He is going to help a few people. He will hurt many more. If he is smart, he will learn to harness his tongue. The Bible says there is a time to keep silence (see Eccles. 3:7). Only a fool ignores it (see Prov. 10:14).

A wise mate chooses his words carefully. Words are hard to swallow later.

A man was yelling at his wife in haste. Words rolled off his tongue thoughtlessly. Finally, he said, "I wish I had never married you." Later he regretted that little outburst. He apologized. They made up. Everything was forgotten— or was it? In the back of her mind those words still shift around.

Maybe your wife has just bought a new dress, and she wants to show it to you. It cost sixty dollars, and she is waiting for your approval. Your mind tells you, *It looks like a salmon left too long in the sun.* If you tell her anything you want, you are acting like an insensitive clod. There is a time to be quiet and kind.

The "let's get it all out in the open" cult can be cruel. It won't hurt to eat a baked potato once a month. It might not kill you to go to a ball game once in a while. Some things are better done just because you love.

There was a time when I always felt the need to talk. If someone had a problem, I had to have an answer. When someone was sick or had died, I felt the need to make mini-speeches. Sometimes it is the worst thing we could do.

Some days your partner will need to have you sit and hold his hand. No need to say or promise anything. Your hand in his will say everything.

Pick Up Your Partner

Communication at its best is helpful. There are many things to complain about. Inflation is terrible, the children will need shoes, war is always breaking out. Our conversations often have a way of developing a trend. Some of us are always discussing the negative. Everything is bad, rotten, and getting worse. This attitude is contagious. Words like *fun, better, interesting, exciting,* and *grateful* are also contagious. If you were in charge of epidemics, what kind would you order?

The Bible has some helpful advice. It tells us to stay away from corrupt communication (see Eph. 4:29). All of us can focus on the positive and constructive. For some it will take a retraining of our thought patterns. We can do it. We will be tremendously glad we did.

Proverbs 12:18 says, "There is that speaketh like the piercings of a sword: but the tongue of the wise is health" (KJV).

Some morning, say to yourself, I can help my mate get off to a good day. I'll put a love note in her purse. I can prepare the breakfast he likes best. I'll volunteer to order tickets for the concert.

You can't control the entire day—nor do you want to. But you can go a long mile to give it a great start. *No one* affects your mate as much as you do.

It may seem silly to take lessons on how to talk at your age. You might be surprised at the number of people who can't. Probably the hardest part to conquer is the ability to say, "I'm sorry." Practice it. The smart partner will say it often.

Practice these words in front of a mirror: "I have been stubborn." "I was wrong." "That was selfish of me." "I won't do that again." "I'm sorry."

These are elementary but good building blocks. The person who can say them truly has a great marriage ahead.

Don't Attack

Jack was the kind of person who thought he could say, "I'm sorry." He and his wife, Bev, were determined to iron things out. When you listen to Jack, you can see immediately what his problem was.

"I am sorry I called your sister a witch, but you weren't kind to my brother."

As Jack saw it, he had apologized. What more could she want?

This is the way many of us apologize. We use apology as an excuse to attack our partner. There is no sincerity, no sign of contrition. By apologizing we only inflame the situation.

When you say, "I'm sorry," speak only about your problem. We are like children trying to hide our fault behind someone else's. Maturity takes responsibility. It learns to say, "I was wrong."

The psalmist said, "I will declare mine iniquity; I will be sorry for my sin" (Ps. 38:18, KJV). Don't drag anyone else into it.

A healthy love will initiate the apology. You may be wasting hours and days waiting for your partner to act first. Whose responsibility is it to apologize? That one's easy. It's *yours*. But you didn't start it, you say. It's still yours. We miss a great deal of love arguing over who started the argument. That is academic. You be the peacemaker and keep your love warm.

Experts in the field tell us only 7 percent of communication is by words.

Can you remember walking into a house filled with tension? The static is terrible. Be wise and keep it short. One day our oldest daughter said, "I don't know what is wrong, but something is." My wife and I hadn't said a word, but the tension was obvious. You have too much to lose by letting it drag on.

Express Gratitude

Many couples keep their communications at a high level. It's great to meet two partners who still talk to each other with respect. They kid around and tease, but there is no meanness or callousness. They are polite and honor each other's opinion. They haven't lost their charm. They practice saying "thank you."

One couple says "thank you" as a regular habit. They miss once in a while, but the attitude is there. If you could meet their children, you would really be impressed. They say "thank you" too—for little things: a ride in the car, when they stop for a Coke, dinner at a restaurant. No one rides them; they just say it. Their parents establish an atmosphere of charm, and it rubs off automatically on the children.

You look at your wife and say, "Thanks for the meal. I appreciate all the preparations." Those words make fireworks go off in a girl's heart.

You look at your husband and say, "We discuss money a lot, but I am grateful. We have a place to live, furniture, a car, braces for the kids' teeth. God has been generous."

Sometimes you will want to sit your mate down and say, "I know your job gets tough. But thanks for doing it for us." Those words are guaranteed to make a person feel nine feet tall.

The Bible tells us to have our conversation seasoned with salt (see Col. 4:6). If you are ever forced to go on a salt-free diet, this verse will be easy to understand. Food becomes tasteless without salt.

Give your partner communication that contains salt. It's tasteful, helpful, loving.

You take your partner by the hand and sit on the sofa. Tell her she is soft. Tell him he is strong. From there on it is easy. Then you say, "Honey, I love you just because you are you." Now you are communicating.

Talk It Over

1. Do you tend to be a positive or a negative talker? What about your partner?
2. When is the worst time to share bad news with your partner? Why?
3. Do you talk about love or just show it? Could you adjust and talk about it more?
4. How good are you at saying "thank you" and "please"?

10

NINE THINGS
YOUR PARTNER
WOULD LOVE
TO HEAR

WHAT do couples talk about? After thirty, forty, or fifty years of marriage, they must know how their spouse feels about zucchini bread, the New York Yankees, and vitamin supplements. What do they do now—sit around and watch their cars rust?

Smart couples will always have something to talk about because they have learned the magic phrases. They know the words that will put a sparkle in any partner's eyes. Let's start off with the big nine. You can add to them as you grow together.

1. You've Got Great Eyes
Everyone likes to be praised, thanked, and built up. Even if they shrug it off and say you are embarrassing them, don't believe it! Praise is low-calorie chocolate candy. We can't get enough, and if given sincerely, it never harms anyone.

The Bible says, "And let her works bring her praise at the city gate" (Prov. 31:31, NIV).

There is no lack of people who try to tear us down.

Everyone should have a cheerleader-in-residence, someone to give him standing ovations, pep talks, and reassurance.

Count any day a dud that you don't take a few minutes to lift up your spouse.

2. You Mean More to Me than the San Francisco 49ers

No partner should be left to wonder where he fits in your list of affections. Up front, we all need to know how much our spouse loves us. We cannot live on hints, innuendoes, clues, or insinuations. We need to say "I love you" often.

Hold your spouse close, look him or her in the eyes, and say it in no uncertain terms: "I love you." Naturally, we need to back it up with actions, but don't forget to say the secret words often.

3. I'll Take Care of That

I'm an authority on this one because my wife, Pat, uses it all the time. If I say, "I want to write away and get this catalog," I barely have the words out when she interrupts with, "I'll take care of that." If I say, "I need to get the Mazda washed," Pat chimes in, "I am going that way; I'll take care of that."

Pat is like a hawk looking for field mice. She is alert for ways to help and pounces on opportunities.

We are the fortunate ones if we have married a volunteer. We are even more fortunate if we become like him. It is more blessed to give than to receive, more loving to jump in and help than to argue over whose job it was.

4. I Messed Up the Checking Account

That might not sound like good news, but it can be. You know you have married a mature person when he can 'fess up to a mistake and say he is sorry. It is amazing how many spouses cover up, lie, and blame the other person.

An open, caring relationship can survive "messing up" far better than it can "covering up" if we have enough trust to admit our mistakes. Breaking his golf club, staining her tablecloth, or losing her racquetball racket are painful

NINE
THINGS
YOUR
PARTNER
WOULD
LOVE TO
HEAR

page
102

but bearable when accompanied by a sincere apology.

The song that claims love is never having to say you're sorry is a little soggy. "I'm sorry" is always in style for partners who really care about each other's feelings.

5. It's All Right—Let's Forget about It

Some people love to see their spouses make a mistake. They merely add that bleep to the arsenal of weapons to use against them. Later they drag out its memory and remind their mate of how they fouled up.

Every partner needs to be forgiven. Often, partners need forgiveness in heavy infusions.

If you are short on forgiveness and long on getting even, maybe you will want to hold off getting married. Take a course, read a book, get converted. Nursing a grudge is the pit bull of marriage. The lack of forgiveness will do your relationship in.

Shirley told me she could never forgive her husband for losing their business in 1987. Since she cannot release him from the guilt, he cannot forgive himself. There is a real chance their marriage will not survive because she cannot pass the forgiveness test.

6. Let's Go and See Your Movie

Said in honesty and with verve, you will set off fireworks in his brain. This is especially true if you can add a reason or two you would enjoy it, too.

The key word is compromise. Smart couples are master negotiators. They know how to make an afternoon of shopping sound like a trip to the south of France.

"Sure, I'd love to go to the mall with you. Do you think we could stop for twenty minutes at the driving range? I'll just hit one bag of balls."

Marriage cannot be an "I win, you lose" situation. Loving couples try to find a way where everyone wins something. Love does not demand its own way.

7. I Don't Like Yogurt

Most of us want our mates to be up-front. Not rude, abrasive, or whiny—just up-front.

Few things are as grating as trying to guess what your

We all need to know how much our spouse loves us. We cannot live on hints, innuendoes, clues, or insinuations.

partner likes. In kind but clear terms we would enjoy hearing: "I like blue shirts but don't care for green ones." If your partner says something that direct, carry him to the living room, place him on the couch, and kiss him silly.

We have to know what our partner wants and doesn't want. It's essential to the relationship.

"I keep buying presents for Marcia. She always thanks me profusely," Ted explained. "But then she parks them in a dresser and never takes them out again. Does she like them? Is she saving them for our silver anniversary? I wish I knew what was going on."

8. I Hurt

Those are two of the most romantic words in the English language. They open the door to our heart and invite our partner to come in. They are not the words of a hypochondriac, but the simple confession of someone who has a need.

A few people don't want to hear about the pain their partner feels, but most of us do. We like to help the people we love.

Many of us, especially men, have grown up denying our feelings. We ought now to open the cage and let our emotions free. The person we love usually will have greater respect for us because he knows us better. Test the waters.

9. I Miss You

This is the one that really bakes my bread. Few things conjure up warm feelings better than this. To know that someone likes having me around. To think that I am special to another person. To imagine that I fill a particular need. It gives me goose bumps.

It's a cold world, and often we think of ourselves as simply another blade of grass on the lawn of life. But when someone says, "If this particular blade of grass were missing, I would feel a deep loss," that will curl your toes.

Slip it in every chance you get. Put it in letters, say it on the phone, make a banner when they come home. Raise their sense of worth by 200 percent.

Words are among the great medicines. They not only

cure and heal but also act to maintain good health as well.

"A man finds joy in giving an apt reply—and how good is a timely word" (Prov. 15:23, NIV).

"A word aptly spoken is like apples of gold in settings of silver" (Prov. 25:11, NIV).

Talk It Over
1. What is a word you like to hear?
2. Do your comments tend to be negative or positive?
3. Do you tend to build each other up or tear each other down?

11

GETTING GOOD ADVICE

EVERYBODY needs help sometimes. It may be advice on hanging wallpaper. Or on getting your car fixed. Wise counselors come in handy, even when there are no serious problems.

Maybe you are one of those who has to find out everything for yourself. Life is trial and error for you. I appreciate that spirit. I also know it can lead to a great many knocks and bruises.

Why Seek Counsel?

A couple came to me once for premarital counseling even though I wasn't going to marry them. They lived in another state and were going back to her church.

The girl seemed impatient. "I told Roger we might just as well get your opinion, too," she said crisply. It was clear she wanted to be somewhere else.

She had a good point. She was also missing another one. There is no end to collecting opinions. *Too many* counselors are both confusing and counterproductive. Don't keep bouncing questions off every bobbing head you meet.

But look at the other side of that coin. Friendly, open advice can save hours of agony. In more than one case, it could have rescued a marriage.

"Plans go wrong with too few counselors; many counselors bring success" (Prov. 15:22).

There is another way to look at counseling. Unless you hear several guidelines, you won't know which ones to break. Not every piece of advice is golden. Certainly not every one applies to your marriage. But it's good to hear, weigh, sift, and choose from them.

Before we were married, we talked to three people about the practical aspects of living together as husband and wife. The first one was a minister with whom we had several sessions of premarital counseling. I didn't like being there for two reasons: First, because we had to be—he would not have married us if we hadn't shown up. Second, the minister did all the talking, and I felt preached at.

After we were married a couple of years, I changed my mind completely. The minister's advice turned out to be such excellent counsel that it still echoes in my life. He gave us practical suggestions and biblical guidelines. They make more sense all the time.

Listen to advice and store it. Some winter you may be glad your larder is full.

The other set of helpful counselors was a couple we barely knew. They invited us to their home for dinner. It wasn't a heavy or planned meeting. As we joked that evening, they dropped little hints of what had worked for them and what had not. No big deal, but it was such an uplifting look at marriage.

Many ministers now insist on premarital counseling. A few want one or two sessions of post-wedding counseling. Don't resist it. This is a gigantic improvement over the days when no one discussed issues. Often the extent of counseling a girl received about sex was merely "give yourself to your husband." Everyone figured the male didn't need advice.

There are other professionals who can give excellent premarital counseling. However, ministers will do the bulk of it. If you have respect for your pastor, it can be a tremendous help.

Young couples are coming to appreciate this counseling. Frequently, both before and after marriage, a couple will say, "We want marriage counseling." It has gained a good reputation and deserves it.

In-House Counseling

In addition to your pastor, there are probably a score of other advisers available for your new marriage. Before discussing them, I should mention the best one: your partner.

Each of us has a marriage-counselor-in-residence. The smart couple counsels each other almost daily. "This is good." "This isn't working." "I really don't like tomatoes." "Red has always been my favorite color." "When we get a chance, I'd enjoy going out for dinner."

Dates for married couples make excellent therapy sessions. They are usually more convenient and often cheaper than going to professionals. The two of you go out for dinner and counsel each other. You tell her how beautiful her eyes look and say something nice about her clothes. That is good esteem-reinforcement. Make her feel good about herself.

She discusses her dream for adding an extra room on the house. This is dream-building and fosters hope for improvement. It is tremendously healthy.

You tell her why a fishing vacation is the greatest. This is your chance to expand each other's horizons.

By going out for pie or a meal, you have changed the setting. You have moved away from the immediate pressures and looked at them more objectively.

Many couples have changed the entire direction of their lives through date therapy. By stepping outside their circumstances, they were able to look them over and make better decisions.

There is one rule of date therapy that should be guarded tenaciously: don't couple it with shopping. Many a husband can't stand shopping with his wife anyway. The very thought of it can wreck a date.

Marriage goes better with give.

It sounds tempting. The wife says, "Wonderful. While we are downtown, we can stop in and look at some drapes." Count most husbands out. Just the thought of looking at material will give many men apoplexy.

Before you look high and low for good marriage counseling, ask yourself if you have checked at home. Don't assume you have. You may spend hours looking for an answer that your mate could have given you in five minutes.

However, using your partner as a counselor has two definite drawbacks. First, there are some answers he honestly doesn't have. A couple can't always know enough to clear up every difficulty. When your lack of answers begins to damage your relationship, do not hesitate to seek other help.

The second difficulty is emotional involvement. Sometimes we are so close to the center of the problem we can't possibly be of help. Then we need another person who can look at the picture from a third perspective.

The Bible as a Counselor

Not all good advice comes from people. Every engaged couple can be helped by familiarizing themselves with what the Bible says about marriage.

I don't make this suggestion lightly. The Bible will give an up-front, honest view of what marriage is all about. It gives practical guidelines that can be applied to any marriage. Don't let the book's age deceive you. The Bible has an open, healthy concept of love.

Often the Bible has become buried under personal opinion. We listen to what people think the Bible says. The result is a misrepresented book. We end up with a cultural view rather than a factual one.

If you want to know what the Bible says about marriage, you must read it. I think you will find it doesn't have the hang-ups some of us have.

Here are some passages you will want to read.

Christian woman—Proverbs 31
Sex—1 Corinthians 7:1-7
Love—1 Corinthians 13
In-laws—Ephesians 5:31

Happy Couples

Another source of good advice is from a happily married couple. If you know a miserable couple, play Clue with them, but don't look for clues about your marriage. Their perspective is different. They have something to offer, but the total sum will probably be negative. Your view can become distorted in a hurry.

Happy couples are another story. They have problems and challenges. They also have fun.

Peg and Bob have a special relationship with her parents. Peg was brought up in a gregarious home where talking came easy. These newlyweds find it comfortable to talk with Peg's parents about marriage. Even intimate subjects are discussed with candor. If you can do this, by all means do. Parents have twenty to thirty years of good experience. It would be great to make use of some of their wisdom.

The same thing is true of other happily married couples. Just hanging around them is helpful. Their good qualities have a way of rubbing off. Sometimes you may want to ask these couples direct questions. Other times you will benefit by watching how they behave at home.

Marriage Books

Early in your experience as husband and wife, it would be good to read a sex manual. There is nothing indecent about this if it is read in a Christian context.

Despite the large publicity sex gets, there remains an enormous ignorance of the facts. Some individuals who are about to get married have only the vaguest concept of what intercourse is.

If all we know about sex is dirty jokes and handwriting on walls, we are in sad shape. A sex manual can be a marriage saver.

Get your first sex manual from your doctor. If he doesn't offer one, ask for it. They are informative and factual.

If you want to buy one from a store, do it later. Often these resemble gymnastics manuals more than love guides. They might be overwhelming for newlyweds.

Other types of books are valuable also. General guides

Certain Christians are very proud that they have never seen a marriage counselor. Some of them have been miserable for years.

to marriage can give excellent advice. New ones are coming out on the market continuously.

Take a Class
Classes are also tremendous aids. If your church doesn't have a class on marriage, start lobbying now. You don't have to take it each time it is offered. However, it can help keep a marriage fresh.

Years ago classes on marriage were unheard of. Marriage was supposed to be natural. Discussing it in groups was considered brash. Now we know married couples can use the help.

Many couples need a place to raise the questions they have. They want to know how others are handling things. Jump in on a class!

When You Don't Need a Counselor
Marriage has suffered from too much romanticizing. At other times it grinds along from too little. Some partners did not really expect the ups and downs, smiles and tears that come with the package.

"I think I read too many books," said one girl. "They centered around the romance and selecting homes and buying curtains. It all looked like a beautiful picture coming together stroke by stroke."

There may have been a few strokes she had not counted on.

Happiness is plentiful in marriage. Not only will it have the joys you counted on, but it will hold many good surprises. The big problem is that happiness is not constant in marriage. But then, none of the pleasures of life are constant. To accept this is the beginning of maturity.

Expect cross words, flare-ups, and even insults. They aren't the end of the world. Smart couples try to keep them to a minimum, but they also know how to cushion them.

Try a little experiment. Place your hand on a table palm down. Press your hand as tightly as possible against the tabletop. Now hit it hard with your other hand. If you hit it briskly, it hurts.

Now lift your hand so it isn't pressed tightly on the

table. Hit it again. Your hand will hurt less now because it has more give.

Marriage goes better with give. Sooner or later your partner will disappoint you. Learn to give with the bumps because the bumps are coming.

A woman with a list of complaints came to see me. Her husband squeezed the toothpaste in the middle. She liked to go to bed at a certain time, but he waited twenty more minutes to watch the news. It was all this type of thing.

Maybe she was extra tired that day. We discussed each concern. Nothing was earthshaking. She wasn't suffering from problems, she was suffering from life. Differences are as much a part of life as flowers, sunshine, and singing. She was a partner who needed to develop a little give. Not every crosswind is a tornado.

We listen to other people describe their marriages as if they were happily-ever-after fairy tales. But what happened to your marriage? Your husband leaves his dirty socks on the chair. Your wife doesn't fix dessert half the time. Your lover goes to sleep on the couch and is zonked out when you want to go to bed. Then we bound off to a professional counselor to find out why our marriage doesn't measure up.

Don't become counselor-crazy. Not every tiff is worth a quick trip to a counselor. The smart partner knows the difference between normal and serious. Reading novels and seeing soap operas aren't good ways to find out.

The smart couple counsels each other almost daily. "This is good." "This isn't working." "I really don't like tomatoes."

How to Find the Helper You Need

It is hard to imagine now, but what if you do start to have deep problems—something you feel you can't handle alone? No one knows if this will happen.

If a crack develops that only widens, don't hesitate to seek help. Many marriages could have been mended if the couple had not been too proud to admit their problems and ask for outside assistance.

Sometimes this is particularly true of Christians. We aren't supposed to have marital problems. Consequently, many try to cover them up instead of solving them. Many of those hidden difficulties are now coming to the top like erupting volcanoes.

Others develop problems and run to lawyers. They have accepted the amputation theory. If something is giving you a hard time, cut it off.

Lawyers make lousy marriage counselors. If a Christian is having serious marital problems, the best person to seek for a solution is his pastor. Without being prejudiced, I really think this is an excellent start. Some ministers are terrible at marriage counseling. So are some counselors. However, the majority are good resource people.

Many ministers have extensive experience dealing with families. Often they are authorities on root causes of family difficulties—such things as lack of forgiveness, intolerance, inflexibility, fear, and even poor communication.

Maybe your minister isn't a good counselor. He still could be the place to start. Ask him if he could refer you to someone. Most of us don't know a dependable counselor. We are reluctant to pick a name from the phone book. Ministers have names and experience working with marriage counselors.

On a number of occasions, I have tried to recommend another minister. Some couples were reluctant to talk to me because they felt they knew me too well. In some communities relatives are thick and are part of the problem. It could be healthy to refer the couple to a pastor across town or in the next town.

No one has to feel hurt or sneaky. In some settings there will be greater freedom if you can get away from home turf.

A doctor and hospital administrator once paid the clergy a high compliment. I met him while serving my tour as a hospital chaplain.

"I have high regard for you ministers. A few years ago my wife and I were having a bad time. I don't go to church, but my wife convinced me to try some counseling with a local minister. He never even mentioned the fact that I didn't go there. He really did a lot to save our marriage."

This open-door attitude won't always be true. With the better pastors it will. If you want a marriage counselor or a psychologist, tell your minister. He wants what is best for you and will refer you to the help you need.

Certain Christians are very proud that they have never seen a marriage counselor. Some of them have been miserable for years. They will never find help. For them the name of the game is to keep looking good while they rot internally. Our compassion goes out to them.

Wherever you go to seek advice and counsel, there are a few guidelines to keep in mind. Even when there is a serious rift between you and your partner, certain rules abide. You have pledged your love to your mate. Now that things are rocky, don't turn and try to hurt him.

Aim for a Solution!

Some partners are angry and so try to smear their mate. They have told the grocery clerk, bridge club, and dentist all about their difficulties. No matter how often they tell it, their partner comes out as the Creature from the Black Lagoon.

My advice to them: Cool it! Your behavior is nonproductive and cruel. This kind of talk says more about the one speaking than the one being charged. Instead, tell a professional or a confidant what the problem is. Be specific, but don't drag in every old gripe and imagined gripe over the past five years. Exaggerated charges only hinder a solution.

Aim for a solution! Some partners enjoy complaining about their spouses. It keeps their mind off the kids or a miserable job. Rather than being like them, look for an answer.

My wife is sacred. There are times when I have not always appreciated her. But *never* have I wanted to make her look like a villain in front of my friends.

When I hear husbands speaking derogatorily about their wife, I cringe. My wife has loved me through storms and sunshine. She is the mother of my three children. She is too sacred to smear. I don't hold many things in life as untouchable, but my wife is one of them.

"Her children stand and bless her; so does her husband. He praises her with these words: 'There are many fine women in the world, but you are the best of them all' " (Prov. 31:28-29).

My wife is sacred. Never have I wanted to make her look like a villain in front of my friends.

If you are looking for good advice, don't just look for people who will agree with you. This doesn't solve anything; it only reinforces your position.

A few even go so far as to seek a counselor so they can feel free to divorce. Having determined to split, they can now say, "Well, I tried counseling, but we didn't get anywhere."

It is hard to get anywhere when a person has his mind made up.

The best attitude toward advice is to see it as part of your search for help. Seeing your need to grow, learn, and expand is at the heart of seeking counsel. We are asking someone to help us see something we couldn't see before.

Many couples can't identify the roots of their problems. We might think we have trouble communicating. In reality, financial debts may leave us too depressed to talk. We might believe we are losing interest in sex. We may actually be too relationally sick to care.

Talking it over can be a real eye opener. Find someone with patient ears, a little experience, and two tons of compassion.

"How does a man become wise? The first step is to trust and reverence the Lord! Only fools refuse to be taught. Listen to your father and mother. What you learn from them will stand you in good stead; it will gain you many honors" (Prov. 1:7-9).

Talk It Over
1. Who do you know that has a good marriage? How would you feel about having them over for an evening and asking them questions about marriage?
2. Is there a class in your church on the subject of marriage? When could you take the class?

12

HAUNTED HOUSES

"BEFORE I met Jan my sex life was, well, active. Now that we are going to get married, I wonder if I should tell her everything?"

Brad isn't the only person facing this dilemma. This is one of the questions most frequently asked by engaged couples. How much do you tell and when?

Exercise Sensitivity
This is a complex problem. Don't assume that because you are Christians you should tell everything and the sooner the better. People are like snowflakes; no two are the same.

◡ Isn't holding back the truth just the same as lying? They are definitely not the same. One night my back ached, and I didn't tell my wife. I didn't lie about it, but neither did I tell her everything.

The person who is just doggedly, tastelessly determined to let it all hang out may be starting an avalanche he can't control.

Naturally, your partner needs to know anything that may affect your marriage. Have you been married previously? Do you have a child? Do you have a serious illness?

Are there legal entanglements that may affect you? Do you have a prison record? Do you have a history of mental health problems?

These facts may not hurt your marriage at all. However, your partner has a right to know what to expect. In most cases the knowledge will only strengthen the relationship. If it can destroy the two of you, this is a good time to find out.

But don't try to shock. Don't exhume every sordid detail. It may be more than the person really wanted to know, at least for now.

Do not lie to your partner. If he asks you a direct question, it deserves a direct answer. But this doesn't mean you have to expound on the subject. If you ask me if I have ever walked up the Washington Monument, you don't expect me to describe every step.

Does this mean you should never tell her or him about your past? By no means. Remember that not everything is worth blurting out.

Because you are a sensitive partner, you learn to read the person you love. Is this a good time to discuss your activities while you were in the service? Maybe it is. Would a better time be two years from now when the two of you are sharing? A distinct possibility. Would the best time be never? Don't rule it out.

Back off and evaluate your situation. The "I have to tell everything" fever may not be helpful.

"I don't really care what his past was like. I know what he is like now." Sandra said it and meant it. Later the conversation may turn naturally in that direction, and she will want to know more. Don't force her under the heat of "I have to tell all."

Barbara should know today. Henry would like to know six months from now. Doris can't quite handle it yet. Shawn doesn't care to ever know. Learn what your partner is like and respond lovingly.

Two Anchors of Marriage
Whether or not you and your partner have a checkered past, there are two anchors your marriage will need. They are called forgiving and forgetting.

The same high qualities that make you an excellent person will also make you a magnificent partner. If you find it easy to forgive, you are well down the hall of happiness. Those who hold grudges and are set on getting even are heading for the pits.

If your mate is vengeful and unforgiving, you are marrying a headache. Buy bottles of aspirin and a football helmet—you are going to need both.

The need for forgiveness will stretch like a wing across your married life. The couples who learn forgiveness will climb like the eagles.

This forgiveness begins today. And it begins by forgiving yourself. Many couples who have been engaged for a long period have participated in some form of premarital sexual activity. It may have been heavy petting or intercourse. It could also involve a number of other sexual activities.

If you have, are you going to let it haunt you? Many young couples do. After they have been married two, five, or fifteen years, they are still carrying this ghost around. They have repented but never accepted the forgiveness of God, and perhaps they have not forgiven each other.

Steve and Renee let their premarital sexual activities practically rule their lives. She became pregnant, and they got married. In their early years all they discussed was how they got into this mess. They often mentioned it to their friends. When their children began to grow, they started their war cry immediately: "Don't let the same thing happen to you that happened to us."

What a waste! They flunked the first test of happiness. They weren't able to forgive each other.

After you are married, sex will probably become less of an issue than it was before marriage. Broken promises, exaggerations, and maybe even an occasional lie may become the patience stretchers.

Don't discount the way you respond to these little things. Many couples could not cope because they couldn't forgive and forget the small faults.

There was a funny movie in which a husband was looking at *Time* magazine and he, off the cuff, commented about a picture of a pretty woman. The wife didn't think the remark was cute. In short order the incident

Some behavior cannot be forgiven or forgotten until it is faced.

mushroomed, and they were both seeing their lawyers.

While you are handling the big problems, watch out. The little ones will creep up and shanghai you. Try to separate the incidences from the patterns. Once in a while your partner will be thoughtless. Don't blow this out of proportion.

Kathy has always been sensitive about the size of her nose. When I met her I didn't think it looked big, but she thought so. Her husband Ron knew she worried too much, so he was careful not to mention it, even in kidding.

One day the couple was wrestling on the floor playfully and trading meaningless insults. Without thinking Ron said, "Let go of me, hawk nose."

Ron didn't come close to meaning it. He didn't even think it. It was careless, and in this case it was cruel.

This bothered Kathy, but fortunately, she was mature enough to let it ride. Her first thought was *You dog!* but she held back. Later she said how glad she was she let the remark bounce off rather than going to war over it.

Throw off the small pebbles immediately. They get flung all the time and are not worth the bother. If you keep each pebble, they soon start to weigh a ton. Forgive and forget immediately.

When it comes to patterns, it may be a different story.

Confront the Patterns
There was a newlywed who had a habit. She kept leaving the bottom dresser drawer open. No big deal. Every morning she gave it a half push and it stuck out about six inches.

Her husband worked hard at being Prince Charming. Each morning he cracked his shin on the drawer. It smarted terribly, but he wouldn't say anything. While one hand held his shin, the other one would politely close the drawer. He said nothing, and she left it open for months.

One morning he cracked his shin for the fortieth time and wheeled in one motion and belted his wife. He saw a pattern in his wife, but he refused to deal directly and kindly with the situation. They could have discussed the problem, adjusted their behavior, hugged, and forgotten it. But because of his refusal to deal with an obvious pattern, it became explosive.

Some behavior cannot be forgiven or forgotten until it is faced. If he leaves his socks where you do not like it once or twice, let it ride. When he does it all the time, talk. If a certain behavior still bugs you, it is not forgiven or forgotten. Fools put blankets over fires without making sure they are out. Smart partners love each other enough to deal with dangerous patterns.

Your home is going to be an open, forgiving environment. Most people who care enough to prepare for marriage are careful to work on forgiveness.

Working on forgiveness is the right way to put it. A forgiving spirit doesn't fall automatically from heaven. If this were the case, the Bible would not have to tell us to exercise it. Forgiveness is not a trait we are born with. Some people can forgive more easily than others because they have practiced it more often.

The Bible merely tells us to stop being harsh and start being kind.

"Stop being mean, bad-tempered, and angry. Quarreling, harsh words, and dislike of others should have no place in your lives. Instead, be kind to each other, tenderhearted, forgiving one another, just as God has forgiven you because you belong to Christ" (Eph. 4:31-32).

Again, the same qualities that make a good person are the ones that make a good marriage.

It is up to you to set the pace. Accept that responsibility. You have an enormous effect on your partner. Don't wait for your mate to establish the rules for forgiveness. If you set a high standard of forgiveness, most partners will respond in kind. That is great news for you.

While you are handling the big problems, watch out. The little ones will creep up and shanghai you.

Dos and Don'ts of Forgiveness

Practice needs to begin now. How are you handling the demands of engagement? What do you do when she is late? How do you feel when he picks the wrong restaurant? What is your reaction when he says something that is thoughtless or crude?

Don't be tied to your past performance. Maybe you

did not find forgiveness easy as you were growing up. Possibly it was not popular in your family. Too many young people shrug their shoulders and say, "Well, I am what I am." Here is good news—that isn't true. Forgiveness is a skill perfected by practice. Because you care, you will be more forgiving next year than you are this year.

Because you are more forgiving, you can watch your partner blossom like a giant sunflower.

Couples can misuse forgiveness, and a few of these problems should be mentioned. Don't become confession-happy. Some partners have a driving urge to tell everything and ask forgiveness. Continuous self-inspection is a miserable, neurotic route to travel. Ed said he sold a dozen but really only sold eleven. Now he has to straighten it out. He glared at a woman in the drugstore, and now he feels guilty.

Everything doesn't need to be confessed. You could scrape open more wounds than you heal.

Also, don't make confession an excuse for sinning. If your mate's forgiveness comes readily, you may grow to depend on it. *What does it matter if I do this? My mate will forgive me,* you may think.

All of us do this sometimes, but be careful. At its heart it is cruel. *I won't call to tell her I'll be late. She will probably get mad, but she will forgive me.* The human mind is capable of devious plots. Some are so clever we are not even aware of them.

We need to guard ourselves from taking advantage of kindness. Too much presumption and we may dull the edge.

Another important don't: Don't use forgiveness as a hostage. Many of us are still childish enough to play this game. Our mate has obviously done something stupid. He would like to make it right and get it off his conscience. We see it as a way to gain something. Instead of generously forgiving, we withdraw and act cold. This is holding forgiveness hostage. In marriage it is definitely criminal.

I am sure you would never intentionally do that. But don't be too sure what a sinful mind will do—even one that is in love.

You will be tempted to think about how you wanted

the kitchen painted. When will you ever get a new dress? He might want to go hunting next week. If you withhold your forgiveness and stay cool, maybe you will get some goodies out of this deal.

There is a basic rule about generosity. When we are kind, we end up the ultimate beneficiaries.

"It is possible to give away and become richer! It is also possible to hold on too tightly and lose everything. Yes, the liberal man shall be rich! By watering others, he waters himself" (Prov. 11:24-25).

This rule applies to forgiveness.

Becoming a Burden Lifter

The key word to forgiveness is *mercy.* If you keep records or are waiting to get even, forgiveness becomes a meaningless mush.

We all forgive, we think; after all, we are Christians. But it is possible for the word *forgiveness* to become a hollow barrel. If we do not forgive in fact, we do not forgive at all. Just hurling out words proves nothing.

If we do not forgive in fact, we do not forgive at all.

Mercy, not justice, is the key. Be a burden lifter. Your mate will sometimes have stooped shoulders from what he has done or said. That is when it is so great to have a terrific mate like you. Your love will lift the tons straight off his back. Do it quickly. Do it often. Do it without reservation.

After we have forgiven our partner, the really hard work begins. How in the world can you forget, especially if the pain has cut deeply and you have bled profusely?

You can't keep dredging up the error, either verbally or mentally. It deserves a decent burial.

Forgetting comes in degrees. There are some things I no longer remember, yet I have not forgotten them. (I hope that sentence will make sense to you later.)

I remember the Second World War (just barely, please!). I know how the Asian campaign ended. I recall when President Truman announced it to the world. All sorts of facts and images float around in the back of my brain.

However, I do not remember the war like white heat. I don't hate the Japanese or the Germans. I don't look for their labels on products and refuse to buy them.

Forget the war? Impossible. Forget the intense hate and damage? Now there is an order I can fill.

Your marriage will never become World War II, but some of the principles are the same. If a husband has an affair with another woman, I doubt that the wife totally forgets it. Yet she can bring herself to the place where it no longer vibrates. It is no longer an emotional issue. She remembers it only as an unfortunate part of history.

If you store memories, you may be merely postponing the explosion. Some memories are good for laughs. Even though they hurt at the time, they are funny today. Not every memory can be funny, but all memories—all memories—can be diffused. They are diffused by genuine forgiveness.

When two partners flood their marriage with forgiveness, they can hardly miss.

Have a fantastic marriage.

Talk It Over
1. Do you hold grudges?
2. Do you often feel the need to get even?
3. Have you found your partner to be generous with forgiveness? Explain.

13

MIXED COUPLES

EVERY partner should know what he is getting into. Marriage has enough surprises without ignoring the facts.

What are the odds of success for your type of union? Once you learn what you are up against, you may choose to go full steam ahead. You are not the national average. You are one couple and must weigh your own circumstances.

A general rule says the more a couple has in common, the better the chance of success. They can have many differences and still be happy. However, their glue comes from like interests.

There are three major areas of differences: religion, race, and age. The biggest problem of these three remains religion.

Different Religions

If two dedicated followers of separate religions marry, they are likely to have trouble. If a dedicated believer marries a religiously cold or hostile partner, there probably will be difficulty no matter what the religion.

Write those two maxims on the back of your hand.

Read them all day long. Most people who ignore them live to regret it.

It becomes a different story if one (or both) of the partners changes. Many of these switches work out beautifully.

Before you get married, resolve the serious questions of your faith. Don't tell yourself you will iron them out later. Often waiting makes it more difficult.

There is more to settle than just the obvious questions. Both of you need to know where you stand in your relationship to Jesus Christ. Listen to each other. Don't just look for a key word or a magic phrase. Discuss the subject and hear what your partner means. Some beautiful Christians have rejected great partners because they never heard the right sentence. Others have married duds who used familiar terminology.

It may be difficult to talk about your Christian faith with someone you love very much. (Sometimes it is easier with a stranger!) Work at it. It is something you need to discuss the rest of your life. You can walk around some streams, but this one you have to cross.

This is both a sociological problem and a Christian problem. Most people still marry within their own religious framework.

Suppose a Protestant and a Catholic marry. If one does not change over, a point of separation has to occur. From a practical side, where do you go to church? Maybe you will go one Sunday to hers and the next Sunday to his. Can you be content attending your church only half the time?

A couple will decide to attend his church at 9:00 and hers at 11:00. It is a possibility. How will you raise your children? Will they attend both? Will they eventually attend neither?

This sounds like a mechanical problem. However, other questions could become more intense later. How will your children be baptized? Is infant baptism important to you? Will it insult your partner? What does Communion mean to you?

You can handle those "little things" later. That is what many couples think. Later they find them completely impassable. Cold water is poured on their marriage.

Bring your differences down to close quarters. Are you Methodist or Baptist? Presbyterian or Assembly of God? How do you feel about baptism, charismatics, eternal life, Sunday school, and even Bible translations?

There are married couples who do not discuss their Christian faith because they find their differences insurmountable. The more you resolve them now, the greater your compatibility later.

Suppose your problem is even more serious. Can a Christian marry a non-Christian and be happy? It is highly doubtful.

As a Christian, you acknowledge that Jesus Christ is essential to your life. Can you be content not to discuss something this vital with your spouse? Can you rope it off as untouchable?

The Bible is unyielding in its warning against the unequal yoke. In the Old Testament the theme echoes: Don't marry a nonbeliever. The New Testament stands just as firmly: "Don't be teamed with those who do not love the Lord, for what do the people of God have in common with the people of sin?" (2 Cor. 6:14).

Before you get married, resolve the serious questions of your faith. Don't tell yourself you will iron them out later.

Different Christians

A smart partner will ask a second question. Are my mate and I on the same level of Christian commitment? Just being a Christian may not be enough.

I meet Christian couples who are miserable. He wants to head the youth group and start a home Bible study. She wants to go to church on Sunday mornings and nothing else. There is a continuous friction between them.

She wants to feed the hungry. He has never parted with a dime. If you want to express your Christian faith, don't marry Mount Rushmore. Every time you want to serve, your partner sits like a rock.

Your levels of commitment don't have to be identical. You will be far better off if they are similar.

When you are trying to develop your marriage along Christian guidelines, don't be a carbon copy. We hear of couples who pray and read the Bible together daily. This may be great for you and it may not. Many couples pray well alone and seldom pray together. Work out your Christian life as it best suits the two of you. Some couples are miserable because they are trying to match someone else's model. There is great width in Christian expression, and you should feel free to exercise it.

After you are satisfied with your Christian compatiblity, double-check your concept of roles in marriage. The roles of husband and wife are changing. Over half the married women are now working outside the home. Be sure both of you have a close agreement concerning the roles you will play.

If you have seriously mixed views, painful friction can result.

In his mind he may be thinking you are going to work. All the time you have been dreaming of quiet afternoons spent making curtains. It is far saner to resolve these dreams now than to try later.

Lifetime situations do not have to be engraved in concrete. Both of you may change your minds later. However, any current strong feelings could use airing. If you don't do so now, you may someday find yourself in a box.

Biracial Marriages

The number of interracial marriages in the United States is on the increase. It still is not a major factor in the total population, but it could become one.

This situation isn't a *problem* in all parts of the world. In some countries interracial marriage is an accepted practice.

Twenty-five years ago it was illegal in forty states in this country. In one state a couple could be sentenced to two years in prison for mixing the races. Often the minister or judge was fined for conducting the service.

As recently as 1967 the Supreme Court ruled these laws to be unconstitutional. It is important for all of us to know how strong these feelings have been.

Not long ago a biracial couple went hunting for an apartment in a large city. At each place they were told that all the advertised rentals had just been filled. Afterward just one of the partners went looking and soon found a place.

The laws have changed, but in many places the feelings have not.

Figures have jumped during the past ten to fifteen years. They have actually grown more than we know since many states no longer require race designation on a marriage license.

There are at least 250,000 biracial marriages in the United States. In cases in which a black and white marry, the male is the black partner four times more frequently than the female.

Several surveys indicate biracial marriages are no more or less stable than the general population. Their divorce rate is approximately the same. Interracial partners may have an added resolve to make it go. They also may work harder to fortify each other.

These statistics do not tell a biracial couple whether or not to marry. They are merely aimed at letting you know where the situation presently stands. You should also remember that we are only a few years removed from official condemnation of the practice.

If you are contemplating a biracial marriage, there are at least three considerations to weigh: the Bible, social acceptance, and children.

What the Bible Says

A few people think they can prove God never wanted biracial marriage. But a biblical objection to biracial marriages simply doesn't exist.

God is concerned about Christians marrying non-Christians. People seem more concerned about people marrying outside their race. If God did not want interracial couples, he was capable of flatly saying so. But he didn't. The issue of what the Bible says is not an issue.

What Society Says

The social issue is as tough as nails. We live in a society that is not ready to accept biracial marriage. It is more tolerant of the thought than it was twenty years ago, but it is far from accepting. Some surveys suggest black communities accept the practice, but there is still no enthusiasm. Possibly other minorities feel the same way.

Several surveys indicate biracial marriages are no more or less stable than the general population. Their divorce rate is approximately the same.

Sin seems to have convinced us that we are better than others. As long as any race believes this, there will be difficulty.

Don't think the problem is merely black and white. In many areas, marrying a Mexican, Japanese, or Filipino is greeted with equal hostility. Some communities, however, accept it warmly.

Many families, both Christian and non-Christian, will find the situation intolerable. The marriage will be more painful than most can handle.

It is a problem we should all be ashamed of. Our deep-rooted prejudices are testimonies to our true nature.

Are you going with a person of a different race? No one can tell you whether or not to marry. As Christians we should be committed to support your decision.

Don't be naive as to what you face. Most will meet housing discrimination. Many will get strange if not dirty looks the rest of their life. There may be considerable subtle job discrimination. Your partner will occasionally be treated as socially unacceptable.

There are couples who are facing these problems squarely. They are married, happy, and well-adjusted. It can be done and is done. Many smart biracial partners have met their difficulties head-on.

What about Children?

The issues related to child-rearing in a mixed marriage cannot be ignored. You are not making this decision for yourself alone. If you choose to have children, they will have their own set of challenges. Can you prepare them? Will you take time to mold them?

These are all heavy decisions to make. If at all possible, it would help to discuss them with a biracial couple. Their experience, good and bad, should shed light on the sharp turns ahead.

An understanding group of Christians would be a big help. Their support and acceptance could lighten your load considerably.

We do know Moses evidently married an Ethiopian woman. When Aaron and Miriam objected to the union, God inflicted Miriam with leprosy (see Num. 12).

Many of us still suffer from a racial superiority complex. It has not passed quickly or well.

There are several specific traps to avoid. Don't go into an interracial or any other marriage just to prove something. A young lady thinks, *I'll show my mother I can make decisions without her. When I marry this man, she'll see.* If you can sense this attitude in yourself, put on the brakes now.

Never marry anyone as a social statement. Don't be a martyr who is going to bring a halt to social injustice. Support a political candidate, work in the ghetto, become a social worker, carry a placard. Marriage makes a lousy platform.

Age Differences

Occasionally, a couple is mixed drastically by age. Possibly eight to twenty years separate the partners. These marriages do not occur frequently enough to establish a dependable pattern.

It is fair to say that many of these marriages are tremendously happy. They allow for the advantages and disadvantages of separate ages.

Simple arithmetic will answer many of their questions. Suppose they marry at twenty and forty. Will they still be compatible at thirty and fifty? What about forty and sixty?

How will this affect the couple's attitude toward children? The time that one of them might spend as a widow or widower is greatly increased.

Not all of these difficulties can be solved with a simple "We love each other." Special qualities are necessary to make this a beautiful match.

Marriage is too personal to merely draw lines. To say this type of marriage will be happy and this one sad is a gross oversimplification.

There is a strong possibility Joseph was quite a few years older than Mary. We can't say for certain. We do know God considered the marriage a good risk.

A couple I knew truly loved each other. Their eyes sparkled, and they enjoyed just being in the same universe. She told me, "I'm so relieved Warren is three weeks older than I. If he had been three weeks younger than I, I

Marriage is too personal to merely draw lines. To say this type of marriage will be happy and this one sad is a gross oversimplification.

probably wouldn't have married him."

The age question has become overly important to some otherwise clear-thinking people. Twenty years' difference may be vital. Two or three can't mean much.

Teenage Marriages

While we are discussing the age factor, we can also look at teenage marriages. Here we do know the risks are great.

There is a myth going around that people a few generations ago married as teenagers. Actually, our grandparents may have married slightly younger than we do, but only slightly. Most couples a hundred years ago married in their early twenties.

Teenage marriage has always been difficult in our society. It is rough to determine which factors make it hard. We can say with authority that the average teenage marriage faces a treacherous route.

The present divorce rate is twice as high among those who married under twenty than among others. In these breakups, age does not seem to be the only problem. However, the high risk of failure is a scary prospect for the young to face.

There are often some definite advantages to marrying at a young age. Partners can mold ideas together. They have an early start in planning their future. Raising children is usually easier when parents are younger.

Possibly our society should not be this way. But it is. And broken marriages prove the dangers involved.

If you are a teenager, you will be hard to convince. This is easy to understand, especially if you have picked out a potential partner.

You probably know couples who were married at sixteen, and twenty years later they are happy as chipmunks. But don't bet your marriage on it. A huge number of marriages do not work out.

If you can wait, do. The "I have to get married now" feeling is better off harnessed. Let your life develop a bit more, and you may be able to handle a healthy marriage even better.

Don't let sexual pressure push you into marriage. Get

some hobbies and other interests. Sex is not enough reason to get married.

Pregnancy is *never* enough reason to marry. If all you have in common is the ability to reproduce, you are both in deep trouble. Ask this primary question: If you had a miscarriage tomorrow, would you go ahead and marry this person? Never marry for security because marriage can turn into insecurity quickly.

Talk It Over

1. How similar is the Christian faith you two share?
2. Is there a religious difference you need to discuss?
3. Are you old enough to get married and stay married? Explain.
4. Is there any social stigma against your marriage? If so, what? How have you planned to deal with it?

14

DO YOU WANT CHILDREN?

IS this too early to discuss children? You probably aren't even married yet. There are more pressing questions, such as which music, flowers, and shoe colors to choose for your wedding. In the middle of all these decisions, take a few minutes and check out some attitudes. They will be tremendously valuable during the next two years—and maybe longer.

A Weighty Choice

Doesn't everyone want children? Not now. There was a time when young couples automatically planned on half a dozen offspring. Today there are decisions to make and alternatives to weigh. You not only have the question of how many but whether you want to have any at all.

There is one decision that has to be made now. If your mate is vehemently against having children, do you want to marry him or her? If your potential partner is cool or indifferent, you may have someone to work with. However, if he or she is immovable, now is the time to ask if you are prepared to marry someone who doesn't want children. This is too big a difference to ignore.

Since this seldom happens, we won't linger on the

possibility. But if it is the case for you, resolve the issue before the final ring is slipped in place.

Other degrees of differences aren't worth worrying about. When I first got married, children weren't exactly a high priority. I wanted to marry the girl I loved, but little crying creatures were far from my mind. After two years of marriage, we had gotten to know each other and were ready for a pink bundle.

This growth is natural when two people are pliable. They are open to make decisions together. Now we have three large bundles.

Most likely you will have children. Whether by plan or by accident, this is still the way it works out. Generally couples have fewer children (around two or three) than their grandparents or even their parents. The numbers have shrunk as the United States has become more concerned about zero population growth. Inflation, housing, and double careers are also making a difference.

This isn't all bad. Not everyone has to have children, and certainly every family doesn't have to have six. The birth of children should be a joy and not an obligation.

Good Reasons to Have Children

We are free to have children. We are also free not to have them.

The Bible tells us to multiply and fill up the earth. Give us credit. We have done a great job of this. We may have flunked the Great Commission, feeding the hungry, and being peace makers—but multiply? We have done a fantastic job. We can feel relaxed and accomplished.

If my wife and I had our lives to live over, we would have children again. (This will come as good news to our trio.) These are our reasons. They might help you, too.

Children have made our triangle of love complete. (Don't ask how a family of five becomes a triangle.) My wife and I greatly enjoyed our first two years together. Being newlyweds can be both trying and a blast. After a while, we started to feel a need for our love to reach out. It needed a third dimension.

This won't happen to everyone. I know couples who have no children and find their third dimension in other ways. They spend their mutual love on young people and Christian work. There is no doubt they are happy, dedicated, and perfectly comfortable.

For most couples this doesn't work. They become saturated with themselves and need an outlet. A natural avenue is to have a child. It is a God-given outlet.

Having a child is a self-fulfilling adventure. You feel you have something to give. You also want something in return. A child meets your needs and at the same time becomes a vehicle to express love. It doesn't sound all bad.

Even if it is inconvenient and even painful, pregnancy is worth it to most mothers. Many decide to give birth two or three times.

Often it means even more when the woman has chosen motherhood in her own time. She controls the births as she can best handle them. But those surprise creations can be real heartwarmers too.

We also wanted our own little litter because kids are tremendously interesting. A fishbowl can't even compare. Windup toys are dull by this standard. Children make a fascinating hobby.

Both of us had tried roller coasters, pistol practice, touch football, and theatergoing. None of those activities was a match for raising children.

Every day they change and grow. They become more complicated. But with each turn, they show an interesting side we have not seen before.

Sometimes it is painful to raise children. They become a responsibility you can't enjoy every day. Most good things are that way. An automobile is a big help and a continuous responsibility. So is a house, a job, and a trip to Denver.

Children bring far more pleasure than pain. There are exceptions to this, but not for most of us. Sometimes we exaggerate the ill effects. Usually they are like a steady rain. But children leave far more than they take.

When a couple starts to complain about the strain, they have begun to distort the picture. Raising children has supposedly cost them this and cost them that. They have lost sight of what their children have given to them.

When the children were infants, we didn't want them

Both of us had tried roller coasters, pistol practice, touch football, and theatergoing. None of those activities was a match for raising children.

to grow up. They were so dependent, innocent, and cute. If they had become toilet trained and sworn off crying, we would have kept them just that way.

Then they started to grow, and new worlds opened up to us. Talking was a fascinating experience. Walking was similar to a tornado. Then the first day of school. We bought Mary a bookbag so large she could barely carry it. Our kindergartner was going to be prepared! (Previously, we had bought her a microscope that even her parents couldn't operate.)

Each age was more amazing than the previous one. On three or four nights we cried. On thousands we smiled, laughed, or giggled.

Our lives are rich because our children have given us their wealth.

Adoption

This is just a start. You can add your own list of good reasons to have children. They are important to spell out so you don't lose your bearings.

All of these same benefits can come by adopting. You will shape a life with your life, concern, and healthy standards.

Because of the present laws about abortion, adoption is often difficult. However, it is done—and frequently. Many couples are giving good homes to foreign and mixed-racial children.

Adopting does not prohibit you from giving birth. A few couples have adopted the first and given birth to the second by choice. Others adopt the first child and are surprised by a pregnancy. Either way can be exciting.

If there are good reasons to have children, there are a few bummers around too. Check these off quickly and avoid them.

The Risk of Raising Children

A pretty television hostess told 30 million people she would be afraid to raise children in this society. She probably was speaking for many young people. For all its benefits, this is a dangerous world. Drugs, alcohol, war, cancer, divorce, murder, rape, robbery, and inflation are each taking a terrible toll. No one dares deny this, especially if tragedy has hit close to your family.

However, it is a bit early to throw in the towel. Our grandparents had plenty of reasons not to raise children, too. Many families lived miles from the nearest doctor. World War I was hovering like a vampire bat. Plagues of grasshoppers had stripped the land.

Then came the Depression. And World War II erased many young men—husbands and fathers.

It can be a tough world. This has always been a dangerous place to live. We can't sit in our homes, lock the doors, and say there might be a lion in the street (see Prov. 26:13). To do this is to give up life.

There are risks in raising children. Most of us think we can't afford them. More than likely our parents, grandparents, and great-grandparents couldn't afford them either. Children are an enormous financial investment. All they have to offer in return is love, warmth, and hope.

Children are an excellent expression of hope. We believe in tomorrow and God's ability to work in this world. If he can use our children to carry out his plan, all the better.

Within reason, your children may help dispel some of the gigantic problems we face. Your child may discover solutions to the need for food. He might find a cure for cancer.

Maybe your child will work in a gas station and never get his name in the paper. But by the grace of God that will be a better gas station because your child is there.

Christ has invited us to be the salt of the earth. Our children can help our world rather than become its burden. With this attitude a couple has no reason to fear having a manageable number of children.

Most of us think we can't afford children. More than likely our parents, grandparents, and great-grandparents couldn't afford them either.

Seven Nevers

1. *Never have children to satisfy anyone else.* This sounds silly, but it is a real issue. Some couples become tired of being asked, "Haven't you started your family yet?" Talkative neighbors and well-meaning friends are prone to say dumb and empty things. Don't let their remarks pressure you into having a child before you are ready.

2. *Never have children to create a work force.* A hundred years ago this was frequently practiced in America just as it still is in some other cultures. Don't raise children to milk cows or tend a store.

3. *Never have children to satisfy your parents.* This is a subtle pressure that can become tons of weight. Resist it; have a child only when *you* are ready. Your folks might enjoy becoming grandparents, but it must be your decision. Grandparents visit the child; you have to live with him.

4. *Never try to make up for your lost childhood.* Maybe you were underprivileged or disadvantaged. Possibly you lacked love and attention as you grew up. Now you want to lavish love on your own child.

Under these conditions, an overindulged child can become a real brat. This type of handicap he doesn't need.

5. *Never have a child to prove yourself a woman or a man.* A few people are terribly confused about maturity. They believe an event will qualify them as an adult.

6. *Never have a child to save a marriage.* Instead of solving your problems, it could multiply them. You probably know a case in which a child has saved a marriage. But many times a marriage problem grows into a family disaster after the baby comes.

Children have been used as a medicine. If the cure fails to take, they end up getting hurt. It is too much of a gamble to take.

Find other help for your marital rift. Then bring a bouncing baby into a happy home. The rewards are far greater this way.

7. *Never have a child because you did not adequately understand or use birth control.* Birth by accident can be enjoyable. Birth by plan is fantastic.

Healthy Parental Attitudes

If you decide to have children (and almost all of you will), there are some attitudes to work out now. Attitudes are more important than actions. Attitudes will ultimately control what we do.

Promise yourself that you will keep your life balanced. Parents are prone to two extremes. One group is self-centered, leaving the children to raise themselves.

Another group is child-centered, and everything revolves around making the child's life ideal.

Both extremes are disastrous. If you have to choose between one or the other, don't. They are both the pits.

The first problem is abandonment-in-residence. Children are left to grow up by themselves.

Have you met couples who were into every activity in the world except raising children? They cannot say no, basically because they don't want to say no. If someone needs a couple to chair the Save the Pebble committee, you can count on them.

It is almost as if we are embarrassed to say, "I need time to raise my children." Yet this must be a high priority among parents.

A woman told me about all the people who were influencing her son. The fact is no one—no one—has as much influence over your children as you do. Not if you want that influence.

Parents have four hours a night plus twelve hours on Saturday and twelve on Sunday. That is forty-four hours. No teacher, television set, or friend spends that much time with a child.

If everything else has priority in our lives, our children will be left to be raised by others. Don't be content with that.

The other problem is to center our lives on our children. Everything revolves around them.

The happiness of our child becomes not only our major concern but often our only one. This is no exaggeration.

Linda was this type of mother, and she was fed up with it. On Monday she took the kids to piano; Tuesday was 4-H; Wednesday was Awana; Thursday was basketball; Friday was a slumber party or some other social event. If it rained, she drove two paper route deliverers.

She had no life of her own. She lived for her kids and them alone. Their wish had become her command. Is it any wonder life felt dull and meaningless?

Such parents often divorce at forty. When their children leave, their world collapses. Over the years the partners have lost all their mutual interests. Now they are alone

Your folks might enjoy becoming grandparents, but it must be your decision. Grandparents visit the child; you have to live with him.

with nothing in common. They decide to start life all over again.

Children suffer from too much neglect. Children also suffer from too much attention. Unhappy parents usually contribute to making unhappy children.

A Parent's Responsibility

Determine you will raise your child for himself or herself and not for everyone else. This is one of the most difficult tasks in parenthood.

One day we were faced squarely with this problem. Our oldest girl asked if she could go to see a children's movie. If she had known what a crisis this presented, she surely would not have asked. Many of our close Christian friends thought that going to a movie was one of the worst things a person could do. To complicate matters, they were highly vocal.

Finally, we came to this conclusion: For us to raise our children to please others was immoral.

The important question was whether the movie was good or bad for our girl. Neither our community nor our church nor our friends could raise our children. God put the responsibility squarely on us, and we had to accept it.

In many cases, we have spent too much time studying children instead of being involved with them. One writer says we have trouble because we do not spank our children. The next says we raise monsters because we do spank. A third authority blames it all on toilet-training techniques.

There are some excellent books about training children. Read two or three and give it up. Confusion prevents many parents from directing their children. Decide on a path and follow it with determination.

Many parents are intimidated by their children. We are afraid they will not love us if we draw lines for them.

Our goal should be gaining respect. Love will be much easier to collect once we have their attention.

Practical Concerns

The number of children you have will depend on choice, career, and health. In junior high school, twelve might seem like fun. High school students might dream of six. Most married couples are now thinking in terms of two or three.

Start off with your picture of an ideal family. Maybe it is two or possibly ten. Keep your options open and go one at a time (if you can).

One couple had planned a neat family of three children. Their third "child" was triplets, and they found themselves an instant family of seven.

If you decide to pursue a career (and most women will), your package of children will probably be a small one. However, this does not have to be true. There is a woman at the local university who has a doctor's degree and five children. Don't try to match anyone. Your preferences and health are the important factors.

Generally women will want to complete their families by their early or mid-thirties. Talk this over with your doctor. The older you become, the more complications are possible for both you and the child. All of us know someone who gave birth at forty or older. That doesn't change the facts. It is wise to consult your doctor before taking this risk.

Frequently couples will say how thinly worn their nerves are after thirty. It is healthy for everyone involved to aim at parenthood early.

Having children early presents its challenges too. Usually a couple is trying to become settled. They are saving for the down payment on a house. Maybe they are finishing school or starting a career. Within these boundaries, their time is limited. Consequently, the family is often just as confined.

There is nothing wrong with this. Life-styles change, and so does the size of families.

Along with the question of how many children, you must ask how far apart in time you want to have them. Probably the biggest reason my wife and I did not have four is that we had three preschoolers at once. We seemed to be taking great risks with my wife's sanity. Since we were also thirty at the time, we decided to restrict the population. (Add to this the fact that one grandmother threatened my life.)

The fact is no one— no one— has as much influence over your children as you do.

This is one of the few things we did right. We had a child every two years, each time in October ('64, '66, '68). My wife has never felt adequately honored for this feat!

It is nice to have children a couple of years or more apart. This has to be good for the wife's body. It also gives everyone a chance to adjust to the new arrival.

Talk It Over

1. Describe your partner's attitude toward children. Does it differ from yours?
2. If you have children, will the mother work outside the home?
3. Why would you have children?
4. Would you prefer boys or girls? Are you equally excited about either?

15

YOU CAN NEVER GO HOME

YOUR marriage is off to a fantastic start. Even before you say your vows, the two of you are building together. You are making careful plans, adjusting your attitudes, and learning about this new relationship.

Marriage will be for you a final step. Some couples eventually separate. Most likely this will not happen to you. The odds are even better if you are both Christians and want to consciously construct your marriage. Numerous studies indicate that couples with spiritual values last longer than those with nonspiritual values.

After you say, "I do," you will launch into a different relationship. There will be no turning back. There will be no escape to the left or the right. You will become two people in a lifeboat. There is no place else to go, so you will sail together.

That is a great feeling. Your job is well-defined. Since you won't get out, you work at making the trip an ocean voyage. Kick off your shoes; open a can of rations; sing together. This is going to be a good cruise—all the way.

Before you cast off, you will want to ask yourselves a few questions. If at all possible, both of you need to answer these. Some of them might seem silly, but each has a purpose.

If you have to answer some of them "no," don't despair. It would help to talk these over and grow. If you answer a large number in the negative, you have a situation to stop and think about.

Are You Ready for a Commitment?
An adult would have to think twice before he entered a room with no exits. Essentially, this is what you are doing.

Don't be concerned if you have some doubts about this. Most of us probably do. Some days you may not be sure which way you are going to run.

However, if you really don't want to be tied down, now is the time to say so. Once in a while, we meet the person who is running and almost never goes home. He wants to do whatever he wants to do. This person loves liberty but has no understanding of commitment.

You cannot be married and single. In order to be one, you must stop being two. Are you ready for this?

"Till death do us part" could be a long time. Orville and Anna McVay were married for almost sixty years. They loved each other like kids. You might be married this long, too. Only those who fully expect to be have any business getting married.

Marriage is not a trial. It isn't a foreign dish to be sampled to see if it is tasty.

Will your commitment hold through sickness and health? Health is no problem. When you can hike, jog, play tennis, and go skiing, there is no strain. When you can love like Greek athletes, why should you worry?

But what will happen when your body begins to quit? Not a pleasant thought, but it is part of the package.

Years ago I met a man bedridden with tuberculosis. He had been there for some time. When the diagnosis was certain, his wife sued for divorce. She couldn't be shackled to this.

I also read an article about a military officer whose wife contracted leprosy. She was admitted to a hospital in Louisiana. The officer resigned his commission and moved to be near her.

Which partner are you prepared to be? Love can be fickle. Commitment does not move.

Plenty and want are also uneven roads. The way of plenty must be the easier, but it isn't always. Many couples split over prosperity. Success can be just as difficult to handle as failure. The multimillionaire Mrs. Horace Dodge said her happiest days were when she was packing Horace's lunch bucket.

Suppose you do become president of the corporation. Maybe you will be professor of whatever. Will the pressures of a full life cause you to neglect each other? Many couples have said no and later forgot.

Pity the pains of poverty. There is a myth going around that claims that hardship draws people closer together. Don't count on it. Continuous debt and financial uncertainty take their toll.

What happens when you lose a good job and can no longer make house or car payments? It probably won't happen. But what if it does? Are you making a commitment that will last through changing conditions and pressures?

"Many waters cannot quench the flame of love, neither can the floods drown it. If a man tried to buy it with everything he owned, he couldn't do it" (Song of Sol. 8:7).

Love can be fickle. Commitment does not move.

Are You Willing to Work at Marriage?

What does *work* mean? To work is simply to spend energy. For marriage to rise to its beautiful potential, both of you will have to pour out energy.

Don't make it sound like a chain gang. Much of marriage really falls together. When love is a motivating factor, it is amazing how well two people fit.

After a few months, some couples are surprised that marriage takes more work than they expected.

A young man who had been married about six months said, "Sometimes I wonder why I bothered. The rest of the time it's fun."

Another married man put it this way: "I'll tell you what the difference is between dating and being married. With the first you are totally frustrated. In the second you are only partially frustrated."

Marriage is not "grin and bear it." Neither is it all "grin."

Suppose one of your early decisions is about having children. One wants to have a child after one year. The other wants to wait two. The choice sounds easy. Love will certainly win out. Or so it appears.

Don't be surprised if it takes the state department to negotiate this one. It may require long hours of discussion, agreements, bargaining, and promises before a treaty can be signed.

The entire process may be loving, but it also can be taxing. Couples do not automatically agree. And when they disagree, that doesn't mean they love each other less. Their willingness to work at it makes all the difference.

Be frank with yourself. Are you used to giving and taking? Have you had things pretty much your way so far?

Working together in an intimate relationship will take a diplomatic and learning attitude. The more you develop this attitude, the stronger your marriage will become.

Will This Be Your Home?

Early in our marriage I asked my wife, Pat, if she ever thought of leaving and going home. She said, "I am home."

For some this transition in thinking won't be difficult at all. Others will find it tempting to look back at their parents' home as paradise lost.

There was a man who dreaded turning twenty-one. He knew he could no longer blame his mistakes on being young. Some hate to get married for the same reason: They can no longer lean on their parents. A new relationship has begun, and they must stand on their own.

Even married couples occasionally ask their parents for advice. If they are smart, they don't do it often. If the parents have good sense, they give it less.

Couples who are not ready to leave their former homes and start their new one are not ready to marry. When you say your vows, turn in your old keys.

Suppose you can accept this fact but your parents can't. A few parents offer too much advice. They are continuously defending their poor child. If this starts to happen to you, don't let it continue.

One young man politely but firmly drew the line with his own parents. They continuously dropped household, economic, and recreational hints. Finally he confronted them. "You have to quit this. You are driving Angie nuts." They didn't like it, but they backed off.

The husband proved he was weaned. Now he had to kindly convince his parents.

Are you ready to burn a cake? Are you ready to hang wallpaper crooked? Are you ready to buy a cheap piece of furniture? Are you ready to make your own mistakes and build your own life? Then you may be ready to get married.

Welcome home!

Is This Purely a Physical Marriage?

Are you marrying a body or a person? It is fantastic to marry a person who also happens to be a body. It is tragic to marry a body who happens to be a person.

Don't take this question lightly. There are some young people who are so aroused physically they are ready to marry anyone.

If you marry someone merely because you need a warm body next to you, you may wish you had bought a cat or dog instead. Sooner or later you are going to have to get up and eat breakfast. What will you have in common then? What will you talk about? What kind of life can you build?

A young man told me about a girl he used to date. She was a beautiful creature. Her face looked like a rare pearl, and General Motors could never have assembled a body like hers.

When they went places, people looked in their direction. He enjoyed the attention. The young man imagined many others envied him, and he was probably correct. He thought about that figure more than he really needed to.

Suddenly the facts woke him up. He found she had the personality of a manila envelope. The only thing they had in common was that both of them liked her shape. This guy was fortunate. He stopped a fancy from becoming permanent furniture.

It happens more easily than we might imagine. Two people have been going together for several months. They have enjoyed continuous physical contact. Thoughts of

Early in our marriage I asked my wife, Pat, if she ever thought of leaving and going home. She said, "I am home."

sex have become overriding in their minds. If they don't find sexual satisfaction, they are certain they will go crazy. They make plans to marry but in reality cannot see beyond a bed.

For your marital health, ask yourself the question directly. Are you sure this marriage is not based on a purely physical urge?

Are You Financially Able to Marry?

There are usually two sides to this question. The first one is: Do you have enough money to get married? The second one is: Do you have too much debt to get married?

Toss the first question around. It doesn't really take money to get married. There may be considerable expense if you want an elaborate ceremony, a new wardrobe, and a honeymoon in Paris. In short, you may *want* more money to get married, but you do not *need* it.

A marriage license and a minister will cost seventy-five dollars. The doctor's fee can be thrown in. Housing should be no big deal if both are working.

Many couples are waiting until they tuck some money away. If you want to do it that way, you are certainly free. Strictly speaking, it takes almost no money to get married. It may take a considerable amount to do it the way you have in mind.

The second question is vital. Do you have crushing debts that could hurt your marriage?

Enormous debts may affect your marriage in several ways. First, they could force you to work too many hours from the beginning. Some partners are working two jobs from the start. This strains a new relationship too much before it has a chance to mature. Marriage is enough of an adjustment without this yoke.

A second difficulty is starting a marriage too poor to breathe. If you start your union with nothing, you at least have a position from which to build. When you start it in the hole, the stark sacrifice can be overwhelming.

College debts might be a different matter. Many couples marry with a manageable loan left over from school. The key word here is *manageable*. But don't be fooled. Many young couples fight continuously over payments on their college loan. Too often their relationship degenerates into bickering over whose debt it is.

If you are overextended (and only you know that), consider working a year until your debt load is serviceable. No doubt two can live more cheaply than one, but *not* if they are rushing headlong into new furniture, a classy apartment, and two sporty cars. Get a handle on your college loans.

If you are old enough to marry, you are old enough to count. Possibly your budget can handle your debts. If it can't, solve these needs first.

Many couples are having trouble. They think it is a communication problem. They are having difficulty in their sex life. A few are leaning on a bottle. Behind some of these conflicts is a financial pressure that is causing the other difficulties. The debts are like a swollen thumb that makes the entire body miserable.

"Just as the rich rule the poor, so the borrower is servant to the lender" (Prov. 22:7).

Are You a Rubber Duck?
When we were children, we had a yellow rubber duck. We liked to play with it in the tub. You could hold that duck under the water for a long time. Every time you let go of it, the duck always bounced up again.

Ask yourself what kind of rubber duck you make. How well do you bounce back?

Some days marriage hits the floor like a rock. You lose sight of your hopes and dreams. You become discouraged and think this thing is a disaster.

At this point your ability to bounce back may be your saving factor.

One evening your partner stomps out of the house and slams the door. You have had harsh words, and he leaves in a storm. While he walks around the neighborhood to cool off, what is going through your mind? You are down. Probably you feel disgusted. The big question is, Can you bounce back?

Will this or something like it be too much for you? Will you take it so hard you can't bring yourself to heal it?

Your marriage is going to have some bad days. How

Sailing out isn't exactly a cruise to Bermuda. You will be better off trying to land the craft you are on.

bad they become may depend on your ability to get off the bottom and surface again.

The most beautiful word in the English language is *resiliency*. This is what a rubber band has when you stretch it. The band snaps back into shape.

Your marriage can break down. It is much like everyone else's. When it does, tell yourself, "We will be back in each other's arms. We are a couple of rubber ducks."

God is the father of sincere hope. Even when things are down, he reminds us of living again.

"So I pray for you Gentiles that God who gives you hope will keep you happy and full of peace as you believe in him. I pray that God will help you overflow with hope in him through the Holy Spirit's power within you" (Rom. 15:13).

Can You Accept Responsibility?

It was fun being single. During college I lived at home and my parents asked little of me. I had dodged the school dormitory, so I wasn't under supervision. Most of the time I did what I wanted.

Marriage changed that, but not harshly or painfully. The fact was, I was no longer free. I had volunteered to restrict my activities. Could I live happily with this new responsibility?

Responsibility is not an ugly word like *shackles*. It is a wholesome word like *maturity*. Are you mature enough to accept the healthy responsibilities of marriage?

You will have to learn responsibility of time. Now it will matter when you come and go. That is good because it proves somebody cares.

There are new meanings to the clock. Dinnertime isn't just a matter of cold potatoes or lost money. Now it is a question of being on time because someone you love is waiting. That person went to a great deal of trouble to prepare a meal for you.

Bedtime means something else, too. You don't stay out till 1:00 A.M. without calling. Someone is waiting and counting on sleeping with you. If you aren't there, your partner will worry.

You are learning responsibility.

Shared money will be a new adventure for you, too. A new husband went out to buy a shotgun. Their budget wouldn't stand it, but he felt he needed it. His wife was stuck with a handful of money that wouldn't stretch far enough.

Spending money becomes governed by something more than self-indulgence. It becomes more than your right. In a marriage, the use of money needs to be a shared experience.

A new wife found it frustrating. When she was single, she bought clothes as she needed them and could afford them. Now there was a new element in her life. She had to check with a partner to see how far the money could go. She was adding a new dimension to responsibility.

This is one of the reasons why thirty-year-olds have difficulty adjusting to marriage. They have handled their own money and time for a decade. It may be a little harder for them to get used to sharing than for younger couples.

The independent spirit often has difficulty becoming answerable to anyone. Such a person is used to walking out when he likes. If he plans to go to the races Saturday, he feels no need to check with his wife. He even considers it demeaning to discuss it.

If you have a potential partner who thinks this way, give marriage a second thought. This attitude is self-centered and immature. Many who marry a partner this irresponsible live to regret it.

Sometimes it isn't important enough to check with your mate. Fine. Leave a note. Tell him where you are and when you will be back. It is the most basic of courtesies.

If you think you are not accountable to your mate, you probably are not mature enough to marry. The same principles apply to performing duties. These duties may not be along traditional lines, but each partner must pull his own load.

A husband in Detroit refused to accept any share in duties. The door was broken, but he did nothing. A pipe broke, but his wife had to fix it. They were not switching roles. He accepted no role at all. As far as the home and family were concerned, he practically did not exist.

You cannot be married and single. In order to be one, you must stop being two.

To become a shadow is to ignore responsibility. You become partners in a marriage, not monarch and slave.

Faithfulness is another basic responsibility. Never settle for being half-married. It becomes a question of total allegiance.

Don't marry someone you can't respect. After you are united, never betray that relationship in any way.

Even in everyday contacts, steer clear of giving the impression you are half-free. By all means, have friends of the opposite sex at work or at church. Be cordial and don't be afraid to joke. However, stay away from flirting. It was fun when you were single. It can be misunderstood by everyone after you are married.

A partner should always be able to say, "I know who is number one in my mate's life." Your spouse may doubt your intelligence, your strength, and your sanity, but never cause her to doubt your faithfulness.

Are You Using Marriage as an Escape?

Marriage makes a lousy Houdini. You may be tied up in all sorts of chains. If only you get married, you think, you will break your chains and fly.

You can't stand living with your parents. Your job is unbearable. College is a bummer and you want to quit. Cooking and housework are driving you crazy.

Are you running away from something? Don't use marriage as a hideout. Are you running toward something? Then marriage is a beautiful isle of somewhere.

After you have settled these questions, you will be able to coast into marriage with greater confidence.

The Question of Divorce

This isn't the time to read a chapter on divorce. Yet a couple of guidelines should be mentioned. God did not intend for marriages to dissolve. He feels the same way about it as you do right now. Marriage was designed to be fulfilling, happy, and challenging. When two people become one flesh, they should stay one.

Are there exceptions to this? How does God feel about those who are already divorced? We couldn't begin to settle those questions in a few sentences. However, certainly love and forgiveness are at the center of his attitude.

Some days marriage is no feast. It can seem barren and hard. But remember, divorce is never a picnic. A person says, "I will get rid of these problems and divorce him." Has she considered the new pile of trouble she is about to inherit?

A Marine pilot said he almost bailed out of a plane once. It had been hit by enemy fire and was crippled. He put on his parachute and walked back to the open door. His head peeked out at the thousands of feet of open air and that hard ground. He then turned around, went back, and landed his plane.

Bailing out isn't exactly a cruise to Bermuda. You will be better off trying to land the craft you are on.

Enough of divorce. Your marriage has too many great prospects. Most marriages work, and so will yours.

The fact is, you can never go home. With all you have going for you, you will never even have to try.

R*esponsi-bility* is not an ugly word like shackles. *It is a wholesome word like maturity.*

Talk It Over

1. How good have you been at handling money? What might you need to change?
2. How much influence do your parents have over you? Is this a concern?
3. Do you tend to brood over setbacks or do you bounce back fairly easily?
4. How do each of you feel about shared responsibilities at home?

16

MARRIED SEX IS FUN

WHAT could be more natural than married sex? Relax, enjoy, grow, explore. The marriage bed can provide one of the most pleasurable experiences in life.

Sex fulfills two great basic needs: to have a good time and to have children. This is the best order, not the other way around.

Let go and simply allow two bodies and minds to enjoy themselves. That is really the primary purpose of married sex.

Don't Worry!
Practically every couple is concerned about how they will act in bed. This is natural, and you probably won't completely lose that concern until the first few nights are over. Tell yourself before it begins that in most cases sex works out beautifully. It will also work magnificently for you. Don't let fears, rumors, and strange literature frighten you. The worst enemy of your sex life right now is too much worry about it.

Two young people in love who do not become unduly frightened are going to have a happy sex life. You can take that to the bank.

This is especially true when you first get married. You won't have children to distract you. Right now the two of you are probably each other's favorite hobby. Your health is most likely robust and vigorous.

The Bible has an ancient principle that is tremendously practical. Hang it up at some appropriate place in your home:

"A newly married man is not to be drafted into the army nor given any other special responsibilities; for a year he shall be free to be at home, happy with his wife" (Deut. 24:5).

I have a feeling he didn't spend the year just making kitchen cabinets.

But aren't there exceptions to this? Not everyone has an easy adjustment that first year. Correct, and we will discuss some of the difficulties. However, the basic principle remains sound. Most newlywed couples are going to find sex enjoyable, satisfying, and exhilarating. By majoring on the obstacles, we often make married sex a labor rather than a blast.

By speaking too often about the "problems" of sex, we may be creating problems. Married sex is fun. Look forward to it as a rich experience, and most likely it will be.

Equality in Sex

To start off with a positive, eager approach, read 1 Corinthians 7:2-5. This passage cheers on the married couple with unbridled enthusiasm. Nothing sheepish about the apostle Paul.

He tells the woman to use her body to please her husband. Would he enjoy this or that? Great! Make him happy. This is what married sex is all about.

When you become married, your body no longer belongs to you. The bride gives it to her husband not just for his need but also for his pleasure.

Before you call Paul a male chauvinist, read further in the text. He tells the husbands that their bodies belong to their wife. No double standard. His body is to be used to please her. Would she like this? Would she like that? He is there to take care of it.

This supposed modern view of sexual equality is an

old biblical view. A woman was not created to entertain a man in the bedroom. Rather, they were made to entertain each other.

Since they fully belong to each other, they cannot deprive themselves physically without the consent of their partner. This applies to both male and female.

Years ago there was an executive who had to be on the road continuously. He could be gone for a month or more at a time. Finally, his wife confronted him with the facts. She felt she would have too much difficulty remaining faithful if he continued on the road.

There was no reason for her to feel like a nagging wife for explaining this. She needed the physical pleasure and security. His body belonged to her, and she had to have it close. Paul says don't stay away from each other too long. It isn't good for either of you.

God originated sex—he thought it was a great idea! Sex is not a necessary evil. God is not neutral about sex; he is promoting it. He is saying do it often or you could be sorry.

This doesn't make it the whole of life, as some seem to assume. Their every thought, joke, book, and conversation centers on one subject. But sex is a terrific part of life and should be practiced freely in marriage.

I told a young couple I had knocked on the door of their mobile home on Sunday afternoon but no one answered. He said, "Oh, we heard the knock but decided not to answer." Then he just smiled. Maybe they were watching Jell-O chill.

Please Your Partner

How do you see love? Is it getting or giving? For a full sexual experience, try to look at love as giving.

Too often we look forward only to getting from sex. This is especially true of men. Sex is something they want, need, and have a right to, rather than something they give. But our sex lives will be even greater if we begin to see it also as giving.

During the first few weeks or months of marriage, sex is often fairly spontaneous for both. There is frequently a healthy fever that keeps the two of you going. After a

Generally, we assume men are more interested in sex than women are. Don't count on it.

while it starts to become uneven. He may want more sex than she does. She may want it at different times than he does. They may not want to go about it exactly the same way.

Each partner is wise to become the happy manipulator. It is especially important to give love. The result is twofold. Your mate will become extremely happy and, in turn, will respond with greater physical love.

When the object of sex is to please your partner, everyone is a winner.

The problem with this approach is that it takes patience and knowledge. Sometimes men aren't outstanding at either one. Many men and some women want instant sex. As one woman put it, "My husband thinks he can swing out of the shower nude on a rope, and I am supposed to run to him."

Frankly, this is how many men see sex. And sometimes there is nothing wrong with it. On occasion she may feel exactly the same. But generally this isn't the best approach.

There is no single way to arouse a partner sexually. Each one is different, and each may be different according to the time and place. The smart mate will study his partner. Discover what appeals to him and patiently make it work.

As you develop this intimate rapport, talk to each other: "I like that; do this some more." Don't be afraid to ask questions. "Does it feel good when I do this?" Be gentle and generous. If something hurts or is uncomfortable, say so. It is an important step toward growth that will greatly benefit both of you.

One evening a partner may not enjoy something he thoroughly liked the evening before. Say so and add, "But I'd enjoy it another time."

If you can get this far and maintain it, your sex life can only soar.

The smart partner studies his mate. "She really liked that; I will do it again."

Generally, we assume men are more interested in sex than women are. Don't count on it. We are people and not categories. Women may suffer from two problems: the constant fear of pregnancy and the fact that men have often been lousy lovers. Some authorities believe that a woman's sexual potential may easily match the man's. To discover her potential, she first must stop seeing sex as a duty or a "necessary evil."

Try It

In order to make love, a couple has to be willing to experiment. Often a partner doesn't know what turns him or her on. He hasn't tried it, so how can he know? Try it. Whatever it is—try it.

Maybe you will need to try it more than once before you know what each of you enjoys. In most cases, you cannot sit back and guess what you will like. Making love is an art. It is a clay that has to be worked. Over time we gain knowledge of what to do.

But what can you do? What are the limits? What is natural, moral, and decent?

To many, sex has meant the traditional missionary position. Simply stated, it is a male having intercourse on top of a prone female. Supposedly it got its name from nationals who knew the missionaries had sex this way. In some dark corridor of history, this came to be known as the only "Christian" way to have sex.

Today we not only know better but practice sex in a multicolored way. There is no moral sexual position. There is no immoral sexual position. The purpose of married sex is to have fun. How a couple chooses to have fun is entirely up to them. Read that again.

The purpose is to enjoy each other's body. Would you like to touch, fondle, kiss, suck, squeeze, penetrate? This is your decision to make. Can oral sex or daytime sex or twelve climaxes in one evening be wrong? How? Does the Bible condemn these practices? Absolutely not. Just because some people do these outside a marriage context is no reason to reject them. Some crooks wear brown shoes, but that doesn't mean I can't.

There is only one absolute law for married sex: Close the door.

You don't need to do everything. Naturally, you don't hurt each other. Stay away from anything that offends

No couple needs to apologize for keeping their sex life fresh.

your mate. But anything both of you would like to try is fair territory. By exploring, you might find some pleasures you never expected.

Some Christians don't agree with this, and they have let me know. A mother told me she was sorry her grown son ever heard such a teaching. Back up and look at the facts. If the Bible allows sexual freedom in marriage, who am I to prohibit it? I have too much respect for the Bible to condemn what it permits.

Avoid Fads

Even in sex we face the temptation of keeping up with the Joneses. We might read a sex manual and find out some couples are doing a particular act. Then we might feel we must do it too or we won't be mature. This is sexual stupidity in reverse. If you want, the two of you can do anything; however, you don't have to do everything.

Again, there is only one absolute law for married sex: Close the door. What you choose to do together is your business.

There are plenty of sex manuals on the market. Some are even specifically Christian in outlook.

Generally, they can be a help. Correct information has to be better than the old collection of rumors most of us heard. Too many in the previous generation learned about sex only from barnyards or strange writings on walls. Reading dependable sex material is far better.

If you want to buy such a manual (and it is a good plan), be careful what you get. For some engaged couples, the books could be more confusing than helpful. A volume of 113 positions can be overwhelming. You would have to be a gymnast to do some of them.

However, after you have been married a while, a manual could prove interesting. After all, there are many enjoyable encounters you might not have considered.

One of the biggest problems with manuals, films, discussions, or surveys is the pressure to conform. We hear other people are doing this or that, and we feel we must do it also.

Don't collapse into this trap. You don't have to participate in every position imaginable. Some are telling themselves, *If that is what everyone else is doing, we should do it also. After all, we are modern and progressive.* That little ego trip is not only worthless but dangerous.

As time goes by, learn more about sex. We read about health, foods, and temperament. There is also something wholesome in learning about sex. Then do what you think you would like.

It only makes sense to study the subject and to study your wife or husband. After ten years of marriage, I attended a sex seminar and learned some things about my wife I had never known. When I got home, I found out they were absolutely true.

After you have been married a while, buy an extensive sex manual. Every couple of years you might want to read another one. No couple needs to apologize for keeping their sex life fresh.

In all sex manuals, use your Christian guidelines. Group and homosexual sex do not become open options just because they are discussed in a book.

A part of what kind of lover your partner is depends on what type of lover you make him.

How Often?

How often will a couple want to have sex? The national average is around two or three times a week. The problem with this figure is that some couples use it as their gauge for success. They think three times is going overboard and one time indicates a maladjustment. Here is another trap.

Enjoy sex as often as the two of you like—no more and no less. Then the number of times will be just right.

In the early days of marriage, sex may be at fever pitch. Later it may have its peaks and valleys. Don't expect a steady line of frequency. After you have been married for several years, you might enter a time of increased activity. For months you might enjoy sex like never before. Few things in life continue on an even pace. Sex probably won't either.

Part of what will change the pace is the difference in drives. Husbands and wives are not always ready for sex at the same time or the same rate. Sometimes they are. During the honeymoon and at times during their marriage there might be a close correlation. The rest of the time, a great deal of give and take might be necessary.

Two guidelines are necessary in making adjustments to each other. First, study your mate. Know what turns him on and what turns him off. Only clods will ignore this. Second, remember, the best love is giving.

We have always said it is the wife's job to meet her husband's needs. The Bible reminds us it is also the husband's job to meet his wife's needs.

This means there is nothing wrong with merely going through the motions. When your mate is ready and eager, accommodate the person you love. This is true not only of women but also of men. A husband can make love to his wife even when he doesn't "feel" like it. Once you begin to accommodate your spouse, you might find yourself more interested than you thought.

There are times when a smart partner will drown his or her drive. Your mate may be tied up in something terribly important. It might be a good time for you to take a walk, work on your bottle cap collection, or jump into a cold shower. Sex often can wait. A mature, loving couple does not let it rule supreme. And husbands, if there is to be no sex tonight, by all means don't pout.

Avoid Stereotypes

It would be easy to spout the old cliché about men being more interested in sex than women. I still balk at this. I am not sure it is true.

Traditionally, this has been the case. Culturally, the sex market is aimed at men. Sexual conquest has been accepted as a sign of machismo. Maybe we have heard this stereotype until we believe it.

The fact is that women have a tremendous capacity for sex. Thoughtful men will appeal to their needs and be all the happier for allowing them to feel free.

Dr. Gale Dunning, a specialist on sexual dysfunction at the University of Nebraska, feels that this is a real possibility. He says, "Women are potentially superior to men sexually." There is nothing wrong with a woman having a high desire for sex.

Avoid stereotypes. Too many of us believe we have a role to live up to. Some wives are far more enthused about sex than their husbands. The opposite can also be true.

For instance, we have often felt the male was more interested in sex because men's sex organs are external while women's are internal. This is *emphatically* not a proper conclusion. In fact, a woman's sex organs are not internal. Go into married sex accepting it as it comes and not carrying prejudices into it like old luggage. Your mate is a person, not a statistic. A part of what kind of lover your partner is depends on what type of lover you make him.

Relax

Don't try to be the national average. Don't try to be the woman you saw in a movie. Do what you enjoy and let it flow.

The sexual freedom expressed in Hebrews 13:4 is absolute. "Marriage is honourable in all, and the bed undefiled" (KJV). Memorize that verse.

Somewhere I heard that Eskimos refer to sexual intercourse as laughing. "Honey, would you like to laugh a little tonight?" That sounds great. Sex makes a lousy science but a fantastic art. If we worry too much about our performance and duty, we are liable to kill our spontaneity.

Some literature stresses the couple being able to climax together. Partners all over the country have worked hard in constant fear one would finish before the other. Unable to peak together, they may have begun to wonder about their compatibility.

Don't take it so seriously. If you climax together, that is a lot of fun. If you take turns, that's a real charge, too. The important thing is that you remain available while your partner finishes—however he cares to finish.

Many times a partner does not have an orgasm at all. More often the wife (but sometimes the husband) will enjoy sex for a few minutes with tremendous passion. A woman then might peak and rescind without orgasm. Her partner may feel frustrated, thinking she didn't enjoy it. The fact is, she was in pure ecstasty. But you can soar with the eagles and still not climax.

I believe other spokesmen have taken some of the joy

Don't try to be the national average. Don't try to be the woman you saw in a movie. Do what you enjoy and let it flow.

out of sex by spiritualizing it. I have to bow out on this point. To suggest we pray before having intercourse seems entirely too serious. Is there nothing natural in life? I have to confess I have never prayed before tying my shoes. I have never prayed before selecting a necktie. And I have never prayed before having intercourse. If I did, what would I pray for? Because there are books telling young couples to do this, I have to raise a voice of protest.

If you are engaged and have not yet discussed birth control with a doctor, do it immediately. What form you use should be decided by you and your physician. A safe guideline to keep in mind is to make birth control a woman's device or pill. She is the one who risks pregnancy, and a couple should make sure she is protected.

We take certain sexual attitudes and practices into marriage. Our attitudes can improve and refine by education and experience. Some of us will be worried because of past practices.

Erase This Taboo
One major sex problem in the United States today is masturbation. It affects and bothers more people than any other sex practice. It is estimated that at least 90 percent of single males masturbate occasionally to frequently. Statistics claim 60 percent of the females have performed self-sex. Perhaps the reader has.

Begin by disregarding every old tale you have heard about masturbation. I have discussed the subject with university students, and it is amazing how many believe these myths. There are no lasting effects from self-sex. You will not go bald, get pimples, lose brain cells, develop a drool, or go crazy. I have both medical and theological books in my library that insist these are true. One doctor of fifty years ago said, "I can look into a boy's eyes and tell if he abuses himself." Balderdash.

Young people who have masturbated frequently will enter marriage with no sexual difficulty or maladjustments. Some problems are blamed on masturbation, but it is not the core of the difficulty. Expect no complications. The exceptions are too rare to expound.

Sometime in your marriage the two of you may choose

to masturbate each other. It can be tremendously satisfying. For many the practice will simply pass away.

From early adolescence up, many of us have participated in some form of lust and mental sexual fantasy. This is probably more the rule than the exception. Addiction to sexual fantasies is harmful. But you can be almost positive that normal sexual fantasy will in no way affect your married sex life. Now you have a wholesome avenue to express your frustrated interest in sex.

Often fantasies and lust continue after you marry. This is true among both men and women. If they are not allowed to go too far, they won't become harmful to either of you.

After you have been married for a while, you might want to discuss your imaginations. In some cases it becomes a good vent for pent-up guilt feelings. It may help you understand each other and make you better able to handle stress.

Rather than act as if we never look at another person, it is often better to discuss what and why. Some things do not need to be said. Rude frankness can be ugly. However, open communication can be great.

Plan Ahead

As your married life routine begins to take shape, make allowances for promoting your sex life. Too many couples become so busy that they fall into bed at night too exhausted to make love. Then they wonder what happened to their interest in sex. In fact, it is almost physically impossible.

Make arrangements for lovemaking sessions. Agree that Friday night you will go to bed at eight o'clock for sex. If anyone suggests you go some place, tell them you have an appointment. They don't need any more explanation than that.

Plan a weekend away. If necessary, plant the children with friends and relatives. Tell them you will do as much for them. Two days alone will go a long way toward getting your head back on straight.

One couple called a baby-sitter and took off for the evening. Just fifty miles away they checked into a motel.

Too many couples become so busy that they fall into bed at night too exhausted to make love. Then they wonder what happened to their interest in sex.

All evening they made mad love. At midnight they checked out and went back home. I don't know what the motel manager thought, but the couple had fun.

Maybe Saturday morning or Sunday afternoon will become a good time for an oasis. Smart partners will carve out a niche.

Couples often go into a dry spell for a while. Both their interest and participation in sex dwindle to nothing. If this happens, keep your perspective. You are not becoming impotent. Your sex life has not died. Almost all sex difficulties are problems of the mind and the setting.

During this lag time, ask yourself what needs to be changed. Is either one of you worrying too much? Are you working too many hours? Is there trouble at the job? Your sex life may be suffering, but almost always the real problem is something other than physical in nature.

Suspicions and Myths

Practically every bard and psychologist agrees: Flesh needs flesh. Experiments with monkeys and humans alike have shown that when all physical affection is withheld, the individual will deteriorate and even die.

Sex is outstanding communication. It says someone loves you. You are important. Someone cares what happens to you. A special person wants to wrap her arms around you, say she loves you and mean it. Someone needs you and isn't afraid to admit it.

No casual sex affair can compare with this. And there are few other things God has given us that can begin to match this type of sharing.

Despite all the information that is available, a few Christians still feel uneasy. They are suspicious that all of this really belongs in the closet where no one can discuss it.

Actually, the opposite is true. Sex seems to be exploited all around us, and still it is not discussed enough. The amount of misinformation is astounding. The number of unwanted pregnancies is astronomical. The increase in venereal disease is epidemic. We suffer far more from silence than we do from free discussion.

Each of us should read the Song of Solomon frequently. Look at its boldness and candor. The author writes about his lover's beautiful breasts and lovely thighs. Nothing prudish about him. Why did God allow this book to be included in the Bible? Is it because he is far more willing to discuss the subject than many Christians? This is a definite possibility.

There are several popular myths abroad concerning sex. It is hard to tell who believes them. Sometimes they are propagated in the strangest circles. Mark all of the following false:

Myth #1: Sex is a necessary evil.
Myth #2: Women have little interest in sex.
Myth #3: Masturbation causes physical or mental damage.
Myth #4: Oral participation is pagan.
Myth #5: All men are great lovers.
Myth #6: Contraceptives are un-Christian.
Myth #7: Most causes of impotency are physical.
Myth #8: Menopause erases a woman's desire for sex.
Myth #9: A hysterectomy removes ability for sex.

After you have passed this exam, go on to the next test. Here are several steps to a happy sex life. Memorize them; your test will come after you are married.

Sex is outstanding communication.

Nine Steps to Intimacy

Step #1: *Establish a time.* Scores of activities are trying to steal your happy sex time. Decide to fight back or it will suffer.

Step #2: *Control your setting.* Make love in some location where you are guaranteed privacy. Trying to love while you are afraid the door will pop open is a bummer. Decide before you start that you won't answer the phone.

Step #3: *Set the atmosphere.* Do you like soft music? Would you enjoy a vase of flowers in the room? Would you like to discuss a sex manual in bed together? It isn't evil to plan your little escapade.

Step #4: *Sex takes patience.* You don't always want a big episode. Sometimes five minutes is plenty and you go to sleep. At other times, early plotting and planning really pays off.

A few suggestions in the kitchen couldn't hurt. A little patting here and there might not be a bad beginning. A good half hour of teasing ahead of time may pay big dividends.

Learn where your partner likes to be touched.

Step #5: *Cleanliness*. Both of you need to get as clean as new sheets. There is no telling what you might want to do.

Step #6: *Communicate*. Is there something you would like to do? Let your partner know. You can tell him physically or vocally. He is probably eager to do it, and it sure beats guessing.

Step #7: *Explore new ideas*. Let your imagination stretch. You might enjoy it one way for a time and then another. Sex doesn't have to be boring or routine. Try it—you might like it.

One couple decided to love by candlelight. When she tried to pass the candle across the bed, she accidentally spilled hot wax on his nude body. It took some of the romance from the evening.

Step #8: *Study your mate*. What turns one person on may turn another off. Feel free to become physically acquainted.

Step #9: *Read a good marriage manual every few years*. The book may not tell you anything you don't already know. However, it might remind you of some things you forgot.

Anyone who has had a satisfying sex life is extremely happy for you. You are about to begin one of life's greatest pleasures.

Talk It Over

1. Do you have any questions about sex that are yet unanswered? Where could you find an answer?
2. Who will you talk to about birth control? When will the two of you discuss what method you will use?

17

WHAT IS YOUR INHERITANCE?

NOT many of us inherited an island in the Mediterranean or sacks of gold from Tunisia, but fortunately we have received some great character traits. A sense of fairness, loyalty, compassion, a sharp wit, patience, and maybe generosity are only a few of the healthy attributes we saw modeled at home. Even if our parents were not close to us, we still managed to pick up from them a feeling of determination or independence.

Parents are not cookie cutters, and we are not exactly like them, but their influence is profound. To make our marriage as strong as possible, we might ask ourselves what qualities we carry over from our family of origin. We might be surprised to discover how many there are. Basically, when children become old enough to wed, they start seeing the good side of their parents. As Proverbs states, "Parents are the pride of their children" (Prov. 17:6, NIV).

At the same time, we may have noted an imperfection or two in the way your parents handled their marriage or other relationships. To make your marriage better, we need to discuss a few glitches we may have picked up along the way.

It's gratifying to hear a young person say, "I want a marriage like my parents have. I don't want to mess up." Often we have heard, "My family isn't going to be like my parents'. They have been miserable for years." Our parents' marriage makes a marked impression on how we will adjust to marriage.

Emotional Atmosphere

There are few areas of inheritance more important than our emotional patterns. How do we get in contact with our feelings and how do we express them?

Try not to think of our parents as good or bad at expressing their emotions. It sounds too much like win or lose. Rather, the question is, How did we see them and how would we like to see ourselves?

Question number one: How did your mother express her feelings? Did that work well for her and the others in the family? How did your father express his feelings? What were its strengths and weaknesses? How is your pattern similar to your mother's and/or father's?

What do you think you have inherited from your parents in the area of emotional expression? How would you like your emotional responses to be?

Mark liked the way his mother let her feelings out. He never had to guess what mood she was in. She wore her emotions on her sleeve, and he loved it. Mark was trying to get to that openness without being rude.

On the other hand, Dee's father seldom said a word. He seemed to bury both his problems and his happiness. She found that frustrating and has decided to become a bit more expressive.

The key word is *adjustment*. We want to consciously use our inheritance in the best way possible.

Question number two: How did your parents fight? Were they pouters or shouters? Were they opposites? Did they fight fair or was there an occasional verbal punch when the other one wasn't looking? Did they sulk or try to get even? Were they straightforward and constructive in their conflicts?

What good pointers can you pick up from watching

them iron out their differences? What pitfalls do you want to carefully avoid?

Question number three: What subjects were taboo in your home? Did everyone steer away from discussing money? Was sex never mentioned by anyone in any context? Did the topics of race or politics or religion cause some family members to freeze up or bust out?

Do you understand why these subjects were ignored or disguised? How might you better address those areas in you relationship?

Communication Skills

Some families are excellent at encouraging open discussion. They prize and respect everyone's opinion. Many conversations are open-ended, an invitation to other points of view. Possibly your parents maintained this atmosphere on a regular basis.

Good communicators are thoughtful of the feelings of others. They tend to be less rather than more authoritarian and tolerate even radical views. Were your parents direct communicators, or did they tend to hide behind evasive terms, mood changes, and attempts to leave family members guessing what they were thinking?

Were listening skills evident? How well did family members involve themselves in what others were saying or feeling? Which good listening traits are you carrying over into your marriage?

When Brenda and Dave married, they came from families that differed widely on approaches to communication. Her parents were taciturn, and his came across like Shriners at a convention. At first, the behavior of each was bewildering to the other. As they learned to discuss their skills, they discovered the strengths and weaknesses of different practices. Before long, they borrowed from each other's approach and devised a form of communication that was healthier for both of them.

Sense of Guilt

Has either of you inherited a sense of shame from your families? Is there an event or a person that overshadows

What subjects were taboo in your home?

everyone, perhaps something bad that happened in the family?

Is there an alcoholic who has embarrassed or continues to embarrass everyone? Is there a convict who no one talks about? Was there an auto accident or an abandonment that haunts some members of the family?

Do you feel a responsibility to carry that sense of guilt or shame?

Every couple should discuss any "ghosts" in their families of origin. Together, identify the source of the problem and suggest ways to put the burden down. There is no reason to carry this feeling into your young and promising family. You may want to spend a few counseling sessions with your minister or another professional to help resolve this dilemma. If not, you will probably pass it on to your children—unnecessarily.

Traditions

Most married couples begin to appreciate some of the fine traditions and celebrations that their parents cherished. Trimming Christmas trees, baking banana bread, singing at the piano, attending Easter sunrise services, watching football games in the park, breaking piñatas, playing carom games or Monopoly, reading at the table—what were the sounds, smells, and tastes that filled your senses?

How can the two of you mesh your fondest memories into a new and shared setting? You may have to compromise. Her family may have opened presents on Christmas Eve and yours on Christmas morning. Be flexible and kind. Adopt the traditions that mean the most.

What new traditions would you like to begin? Keep your mind open for practices that will give your marriage and family its own special identity.

Special Gifts

Each family passes down its peculiar gifts, talents, and interests. Often they include hobbies, such as woodworking, music, or writing. However, they also may consist of patience, dedication, love for children, faith, hard work, loyalty, or curiosity.

Take stock and list three or four gifts that your parents have handed down to you. Thank God for members of your family. You may find this to be a freeing experience that allows you to accept the natural contributions you have received.

Adolescents frequently look for some way to rebel against their parents. This could be a good time to celebrate your similarities with the ones who nurtured you.

For some, this exercise will permit us to be as thankful for our parents as Paul was for the Philippian Christians. With him, we can say, "I thank my God every time I remember you" (Phil. 1:3, NIV).

Problem Solving

Did you discuss problems and ready solutions together? Many families have poor problem-solving techniques. Often we ignore problems until they become critical and demand emergency attention. While that approach works to a point, we sacrifice the luxury of careful thought, adequate input, and shared support. Some problems are too important to waste on rash decision making.

Possibly problems were never shared because parents did not want to disturb the children. Consequently, children are frequently frustrated and confused, sensing that there is trouble but not understanding the forces at work.

Resolve that finances, health, decorating, vacations, ministry, and other important decision making will be a joint effort. Create schemes for managing problem solving. Draw from your parents' examples and improve on them.

Faith

Do your parents feel free in expressing their faith? To each other? To others? How do they work out their faith in Christ in their daily lives? What were the strong points of their spiritual experience over the years?

How will their faith—or lack of faith—serve as building blocks in your worship and service together?

Learning from Suffering

When your mother is sick, how does she act? What does a cold do to her personality? If she is laid up for a couple

Resolve that finances, health, decorating, vacations, ministry, and other important decision making will be a joint effort.

of days, does this make her mellow and mild or grouchy and grim? What about your dad?

If your family were to experience a tragedy—a fatal accident or a terminal illness—how are its members most likely to react? What physical, spiritual, or personal resources are they most apt to call on?

Do any members of your family like to suffer? A strange question? Not always. What does that person gain from suffering? Is there any trickle-down effect to your personality?

Are there any good examples of people who handle suffering well in your family? You might want to share those with the person you are going to marry.

Experiences of Love

How would you describe the love between your parents? How has it differed over the years?

Some parents are expressive and demonstrate their love frequently, while others are quiet and reserved. Has your family been vocal about caring for its members? Are they exuberant, with a great deal of hugging and holding and wrapping of arms? Or do their actions leave you to wonder how much they really do care?

At this point in your relationship, how would you describe your level of showing affection? Is it simply an understanding or an aura? Do you talk about love? Do you find physical contact easy? Are you good at doing things to show your love?

What have you most appreciated about the love your parents have experienced?

After you have taken the time to draw from the best qualities of each family of origin, sum up the situation with some observations. How do your two families differ at critical points? What do you look forward to receiving from your partner and his or her family in character traits?

Talk It Over

1. Take a few minutes to review the discoveries you made about each other as you answered the questions in this chapter.

18

QUICK
TIPS

THERE was a baseball player who could handle hard-line drives like an apple picker. He was fast and accurate. But soon the other team started bunting softly toward him. With these easy grounders, he looked as uncoordinated as a dislocated octopus.

Don't work on the big questions and flunk the little ones. Here are fifteen quick, everyday tips.

Never Give Up Saying "Thank You"
Familiarity rots a marriage. After a short time, it becomes easy to give up on common courtesy. Yet we manage to remain polite to the mailman, waitress, and saleslady. So promise your marriage you will never unplug "please" and "thank you."

Be Dedicated to a Double Bed
A movie star was asked how he could stay married for so long while other actors divorced so easily. He said, "It's hard to stay mad when the two of you sleep in a double bed."

Health makes it necessary for some people to have twin beds. Anything short of that, stay in a double. Some of my married friends say they can't sleep next to someone. Think of what they are missing.

Keep Secrets
Not the big, important secrets but the little, "who cares" type. Every person has to have some private life. Don't press to know everything your partner does at work or home. Don't always want to know who was on the phone.

One husband dreaded coming home after work. He knew he faced an interrogation. What happened today? Were you busy? When is Stella's baby due? Asking too many questions is pressing too hard. Relax and let your mate tell what he wants.

Exaggerate
Tell your wife she looks terrific. Terrific probably isn't the exact word, but marriage isn't a vocabulary quiz.

Many times you don't want your mate to be frank, and you might as well admit it. I am learning to ask my wife to exaggerate. I will say, "How do you like the way I painted the cabinet? Lie to me. Say it's nice. I'm too tired to take criticism." My wife then tries to stretch every good thing she can. Next week I'll repaint it. A husband starts telling his wife how great her dress is. Both of you know you are exaggerating, but she still eats it up.

Do Your Partner's Duty
Once in a while, give your partner the big surprise. He thinks he will have to rake the front yard when he comes home. What a lift when he finds it done!

The wife gets home after a hard day and finds the dishes clean, the living room picked up, or the hall vacuumed. Little acts just say someone cares. It can really light up a mate's life.

Start Loving in the Kitchen
Don't make loving a time or a place. If you are heading for the bedroom, begin early and start in the kitchen. A pat here and a stroke there. By the time you get through four rooms in the house, you will both be ready.

Allow Plenty of Private Time

I love Friday night basketball games. Once a week my family goes to the game and I stay home alone. The living room is all mine. If there is something good on television, I can watch it without moans or groans. I read the newspaper, a couple of magazines . . . Basketball is becoming my favorite absentee sport.

It is easy to smother your partner. Some spouses feel that doing so is a sure sign of their love. Smart partners give enough breathing room to keep everyone healthy.

Make time when she can go shopping alone. If you have only one car, let her take it to get away. Let her belong to a bowling league without you.

Too much private time is probably a lousy idea. A small dose is a great idea.

It's hard to stay mad when the two of you sleep in a double bed.

Do Something Once a Week You Don't Like

Put her favorite record on even if you think it sounds like broken dishes. Play a game she likes even if it is tiddlywinks. Don't wait to be asked. Suggest it to her just because you know it will make her happy.

Be a Fair Fighter

Sometimes you are going to have an exchange of words. There are certain ground rules to make it a clean fight:

1. *Stay with the problem.* Don't bring in other complaints. They only cloud the issue.

2. *Stay out of the archives.* Don't drag up old arguments that keep the wounds open. It is unfair to mention last year's vacation if it is an unhappy memory.

3. *Stay away from in-laws.* If you are upset about the budget, don't use this as an excuse to take a jab at her sister. Keep it within bounds.

4. *Stay away from "never" and "always."* Some of the world's worst sentences are: "You never help me"; "You are always late"; "You never say anything kind"; "You are always complaining." By stretching the facts too far, you make solutions difficult.

5. *Never become physical.* Don't push. Even nudging can quickly get out of hand.

6. *Aim for a conclusion.* What can you do about it? How can you improve the situation? Just getting it out in the open is not enough. Let's do something.

7. *Never fight late at night.* When you are tired, you can't think as well. Bring it up tomorrow.

Be Nice to Your Partner's Friends
It is hard to like everyone, but you can be kind. Some of your friends may not be charming. If a person means something special to your spouse, make him feel as welcome as Santa Claus in December.

Never Kiss Her in the Ear
The only time my wife ever hit me was when I kissed her in the ear. I was teasing her, and about the third time I kissed her in the ear, she pivoted with a deadly blow and rang my bell.

Later she kissed me in the ear and showed me the problem. It sounds like a freight train hitting a brick wall.

There is a thin line between playful teasing and pure aggravation. Learn the difference now. Many of us like to be teased. We enjoy the attention and know our partner cares. None of us likes to be aggravated.

Don't Do Private Things in Public
It is tasteless for a couple to embarrass friends or visitors. Have you ever seen a couple pawing and nibbling on each other in a store, theater, or park? Mature people control their passions in public.

The same can be said of arguing. It is fine for a couple to disagree in public. They can take opposite sides of an issue and debate forever. It is another matter to blatantly correct each other. Bawling out a spouse in public remains ugly.

Stay Clean
When you marry, the two of you may have different standards of cleanliness. You can adjust quickly. The best guideline: No one has ever been too clean. Baths and brushed teeth can hardly be overdone.

Never Flaunt Your Intelligence

There is nothing wrong with having brains, only with throwing them around. An intelligent and secure person doesn't have to prove it.

If one partner is constantly overwhelming the other, an unhealthy relationship can soon result. Don't make marriage a physics exam.

Suggest Nice Surprises for
Your Partner's Parents

This is an extra mile you don't have to go—just something kind and thoughtful.

More Quick Tips

The Bible is packed with quick tips for married couples. Search the Scriptures and find a wealth of practical advice. I'll list just a few.

"Above all else, guard your affections. For they influence everything else in your life" (Prov. 4:23).

"Drink from your own well, my son—be faithful and true to your wife" (Prov. 5:15).

"A beautiful woman lacking discretion and modesty is like a fine gold ring in a pig's snout" (Prov. 11:22).

"A worthy wife is her husband's joy and crown; the other kind corrodes his strength and tears down everything he does" (Prov. 12:4).

"It is better to eat soup with someone you love than steak with someone you hate" (Prov. 15:17).

"Love forgets mistakes; nagging about them parts the best of friends" (Prov. 17:9).

"A father can give his sons homes and riches, but only the Lord can give them understanding wives" (Prov. 19:14).

"Better to live in the desert than with a quarrelsome, complaining woman" (Prov. 21:19).

"A constant dripping on a rainy day and a cranky woman are much alike! You can no more stop her complaints than you can stop the wind or hold onto anything with oil-slick hands" (Prov. 27:15-16).

"And you husbands, show the same kind of love to

Never fight late at night. When you are tired, you can't think as well. Bring it up tomorrow.

your wives as Christ showed to the church when he died for her" (Eph. 5:25).

"These older women must train the younger women to live quietly, to love their husbands and their children, and to be sensible and clean minded, spending their time in their own homes, being kind and obedient to their husbands, so that the Christian faith can't be spoken against by those who know them" (Titus 2:4-5).

Talk It Over
1. What additional tips have you heard about marriage?
2. What couple do you know who are good models in their marriage? What makes them excellent examples?

19

WEDDINGS AND HONEYMOONS

THE first purpose of a wedding is marriage. The second purpose is a social function. Don't get these two confused. Plan a wedding you can enjoy.

To keep your wedding where you want it, remind yourself of several guidelines.

Five Steps to a Great Wedding

1. *Plan the wedding you want.* Don't give in to the pressure of keeping up with the Joneses. If you want a forty-pound cake and tons of flowers, by all means have them. But if you want to get married in a living room with a collection of eight relatives, please do that.

Let the wedding be an expression of your personalities. Make it a fulfillment of your dreams. When it is a forced exercise, a wedding can easily become a tension-filled hassle.

In our culture a wedding is usually the bride's domain. Often her parents pay for the ceremony, or she does alone, or the new partners pay together. In any case, she normally decides what she would like. Because they love each other, the partners will come to reasonable agreement as to what suits them both.

2. *A word to the new husband: Go along.* Most women

have been dreaming about their wedding for years. Whether they want it simple or ornate, they often have the mental picture set in stone. Let it be her wedding. In many cases all the groom has to do is show up. If he keeps saying yes through the entire service, he will end up married.

The bride needs to be sensitive to your personality. If it might give you a stroke to memorize your vows, then let her know. Reciting a poem may not be something you can handle.

If she has a set dream, try your best not to upset it. There is nothing as lovely as a happy bride.

3. *Hope for good support from the bride's parents.* In most cases they go as far as they can. But sometimes they are determined to make it their marriage. A few feel that if they are paying for it, they call the shots. That's too bad. It can then become a social occasion aimed primarily at pleasing the parents and their friends.

I married a couple who wanted a simple wedding. They wanted a few friends in the church, no reception, and an immediate departure for a camping trip. This was their life-style. They were a jeans couple and wanted to stay that way. Soon their parents were taking over and making it a ceremony neither of them wanted.

Most parents are extremely helpful and understanding. If yours are that way, kiss them twice a day.

4. *Keep your plans within your grasp.* Some brides are making dresses and rewriting music at the last moment, and their weddings become nightmares. A few weddings become too much of a headache. Feelings may become strained and arguments erupt. Don't stretch your plans beyond what you can comfortably manage.

Our present wedding practices are not eternal. We didn't always do it this way. It isn't pagan to change the music. Many of my old friends in the Midwest were not married in churches. In those days it didn't seem necessary or proper to have a wedding outside a home.

God's blessing isn't restricted to church weddings. He doesn't confuse the wedding and the social function. The wedding of a good-looking couple named Isaac and Rebekah is recorded in the Old Testament. In that case

WEDDINGS
AND
HONEY-
MOONS

page
184

the marriage ceremony was simple. He took her to his tent (Gen. 24:67).

The color dress the bride wears is not dictated by God either. If you want to wear a white dress, by all means do it. Your clothing doesn't have to be a commentary on your virtue. That would be cruel.

5. *Alternatives to the traditional ceremony are good possibilities.* Most clergymen will go along. You may not want an underwater ceremony in scuba suits as one couple had. Your first choice will probably not be to marry on roller skates, even if you want to get off to a rolling start.

But there are other alternatives. Would you enjoy a wedding in a garden? Would you like it as part of the morning worship service? How about in a living room? In a judge's chambers? What is your dream? Feel free to try to make it a reality.

Whatever your plans, a few people should be told immediately. Let your parents know what you have in mind. When you say the word *wedding,* they may be picturing a completely opposite scene. They may need time to absorb your idea.

Let the wedding be an expression of your personalities. Make it a fulfillment of your dreams.

Arrangements with the Minister

As soon as possible, notify the minister (or judge). Don't assume he will be available. Clear the date and reserve the building if necessary. Lay out your plan and let the minister know what you have outlined. Don't assume he will do it your way or read your prayer until you ask him.

Most ministers have a pet peeve. (I don't like flash cameras and amateur photographers after the processional.) Ask if there are any practices he would rather you didn't do. Ministers aren't bashful.

To take a minister for granted is both rude and unwise.

Do you want a second minister to help with the service? This is often done, but again the resident pastor should be contacted early. It is a little like planning a party at someone's house without telling him.

A very few couples want to elope and tell their parents later. Think that over at least twice before you do it. Some parents wouldn't care—they might even enjoy it. But most would feel hurt. Don't start off your marriage with relatives confused and crushed.

If you are concerned about the predominant etiquette, buy a book on the subject. The most important guideline is to be polite and considerate.

Check the Prices
However your plans develop, avoid financial distress. Don't hope for your parents to pay for a wedding they can't afford. You have to evaluate the situation by communicating with them. At the same time, do not hurt yourself financially. A newlywed couple doesn't need a thousand- or two-thousand-dollar debt for a wedding gift.

Before your plans are firm, check out the prices. Catering, flowers, and photographers may cost more than you expected. If you talk to couples who were married five or ten years ago, the figures they give you probably will be far off. The best route is to find out for yourself.

Happy Honeymoon
What will happen when the ceremony is over? The smart couple will give careful thought to the honeymoon that follows. Just a few preparations can make it the pleasant dream you hoped it would be.

Ask yourself some basic questions. Where are you going to go and how far? Don't make vague plans like, "We are going to Kansas City." How far is it? Where will you stay?

Make a reservation for the first night and make it fairly close. After weeks of planning a marriage and a couple of hectic days, you don't need a long trip the first day. Thirty minutes to an hour is plenty of traveling time. On the second day you can head for a faraway enchanted oasis.

Imagine yourself tired, emotionally exhausted, and worn out from a three-hour ride. You drive into an area and start looking for a room. "No vacancy" signs glare out like pinball machines. It isn't the best atmosphere in which to start a honeymoon.

How long has it been since you ate? Except for cake, some couples haven't had a bite since breakfast. This only adds to your exhaustion. After you check into your room, you might want to freshen up and visit a nearby restaurant. A short pause here is a good investment.

When you come back to the room, you might even want to take a thirty-minute nap. Not everyone needs it, so communicate. Respect for your partner has to be paramount.

Will you begin your sexual pleasure now? Most couples do, but a few don't. More than one bride doesn't wake up until the next morning. Don't be too concerned. Honeymoons, despite their joy, are unpredictable.

Before you begin sex, both partners should take time to get prepared. Bathing seems the most appealing route. You will want to be sure birth control measures are in order.

Do you want to see each other completely nude the first night? Some do and some don't. Don't force the issue and try not to shock each other.

There is no need for shame. Your lover will love your body. Relax. Enjoy.

There is also no demand to become an exhibitionist. Aim for both good taste and gentleness. As time goes on, you will feel freer to express yourself. If you want her to take more off, quietly help her. If she resists, make no commotion but back off. She will get used to the idea as time goes by.

Your first night is at best just an introduction. Even greater pleasure is waiting.

No Comedians

If you have a terrific sense of humor, this would be a good time to keep it down. Trying to shock your new partner is not the route to honeymoon bliss.

One couple checked into an old hotel and started their mating ritual. The nervous young lady went into the bathroom and was soon in the tub. After a few minutes something overhead caught her attention. There was her husband's head stuck through the transom with a smile like a silly alligator.

Their marriage has lasted for thirty years, but the little transom trick isn't the reason.

Another nervy husband told his new bride not to worry about her negligee since he had secretly gotten one for her. She didn't know what else to say but thank you. He said, "Here it is" and opened both his empty hands. The frightened girl didn't know whether to scream or run. Somehow their marriage worked out, too.

Many funny honeymoon stories will have to go untold. Most were better left undone. Be a lover on your honeymoon; you can be a comedian later.

When the lovemaking begins, what you learned from the sex manual will come in handy. As we said earlier, get one from your doctor. Our society talks so much about sex, and yet many know so little about it.

Making Love

Whatever your first sexual experience is like, certain principles apply. Make love, don't just take love. There is a degree of selfishness involved. In most cases if you make love you'll receive back all the pleasure you can handle.

If either or both of you fail to reach full arousal, don't become concerned. Many couples are not able to reach a climax the first night. Most do by the end of the honeymoon, but not all.

An extremely small number become completely disillusioned during the honeymoon and are turned off at the prospect of sex. Sometimes they find it painful, frustrating, even dull. The tiny percentage who experience this should not despair. Good sex is worth developing.

Don't grade your sex ability by the first night. It may be bliss or a disappointment. Often the second night is the one you were looking for.

If the first night is particularly awkward, you might just want to caress each other with your hands. This has two advantages. First, it provides an expression of love until you can get full sexual intercourse into operation. Second, once you relax and decide to do this, you might find yourself having complete sexual intercourse.

Your first night is at best just an introduction. Even greater pleasure is waiting.

Both individuals should know this might be a painful experience for the bride. Her doctor may have made some simple adjustments to reduce this. Either way, be gentle, patient, and understanding.

You are now becoming one flesh. This is the height of Christian marriage. God is pleased. This is not a naughty little necessity. It is a zenith. A rhapsody.

"That the husband and wife are one body is proved by the Scripture which says, 'A man must leave his father and mother when he marries, so that he can be perfectly joined to his wife, and the two shall be one' " (Eph. 5:31).

Whether your honeymoon is a couple of days or a couple of weeks, try to make it relaxing, unhurried, and carefree. Be sure lovemaking and getting acquainted are the main goals. Trying to get to the coast and back in three days is taboo. (If you live only thirty miles from the coast, it sounds like a good idea.)

A little sightseeing is in order, but not much. Under the best of conditions, it grows tiring to read plaques or climb towers. During the honeymoon, it can grow maddening.

Don't try to save money by renting a room with kitchen facilities. She can hardly wait to cook, but this isn't the place to start if you want more time together. Usually the fewer distracting responsibilities, the better.

But do eat. This may sound strange, but the hours have a way of becoming confused. You probably will sleep in late, and it is easy to skip meals here and there. Before long, you are weaker than you thought. Eat regular meals and eat well.

Most couples aren't up to taking anyone along. Forget "Let's take Mother and show her the Rockies." A few newlyweds feel pressed to take a child with them. Think this one over twice, and then don't.

If your honeymoon is not overly busy and fairly carefree, you will probably look back on it as one of the happiest times in life. One of the great investments of life is to build memories.

A honeymoon can't last forever, but it is an excellent way to get started.

A honeymoon can't last forever, but it is an excellent way to get started.

Talk It Over

1. Where would you like to go for your honeymoon?
2. Have you explained your wedding plans to your parents? How did they react?

3. Have you contacted the minister? Are you in basic agreement about the date and style of wedding?
4. Do you know the laws in your state about acquiring a marriage license?

WEDDINGS
AND
HONEY-
MOONS

page
190